The Journey of Womanhood

◇◇◇

The Journey of Womanhood
Copyright © 2021 by Cathy Ify Elebo

All rights reserved. No part of this publication may be reproduced, distributed, or transmitted in any form or by any means, including photocopying, recording, or other electronic or mechanical methods, without the prior written permission of the publisher or author, except in the case of brief quotations embodied in critical reviews and certain other noncommercial uses permitted by copyright law.

Although every precaution has been taken to verify the accuracy of the information contained herein, the author and publisher assume no responsibility for any errors or omissions. No liability is assumed for damages that may result from the use of information contained within.

Library of Congress Control Number: 2021910827
ISBN-13:   Paperback: 978-1-64749-477-3
              ePub: 978-1-64749-478-0

Printed in the United States of America

GoToPublish LLC
1-888-337-1724
www.gotopublish.com
info@gotopublish.com

The Journey of Womanhood

Cathy Ify Elebo

The book is dedicated to the Two Hundred and Seventy-Six (276) girls that were kidnapped from "Government Secondary School Chibok, Bornu State" in Nigeria on April 14, 2014, by the militant men Boko Haram.

Preface

The journey of womanhood is written in remembrance of the female students who were kidnapped from the Government Secondary School in the town of Chibok in Borno State of Nigeria in 2014 by the "Boko Haram" group – some cultural bond men who were protesting against girls receiving modern education. These men feel that providing women with education is worthless because women are not created like men. The men would therefore do everything to convince women to hate themselves.

The girls that were kidnapped were raped, brutalized, enslaved and forced to a life they never dreamt of. Their parents were grief-stricken and the world stood appalled as these girls were swept into the uncharted heart of lake and forest. They battled drowning, starvation, wild animals and the young girls came to know the African mystical, luminous spirits. All these made the writer to remember the poem by William Butler Yeats, "The Second Coming" that gave the world "Stony Sleep" and "Vexed to nightmare by a rocking cradle" which says:

> Turning and turning in the widening gyre
> The falcon cannot hear the falconer;

> Things fall apart; the centre cannot hold;
> Mere anarchy is loosed upon the world,
> The blood-dimmed tide is loosed, and everywhere
> The ceremony of innocence is drowned;
> The best lack all conviction, while the worst
> Are full of passionate intensity.

This writer believes the battle is all over the world, but the battle also resides in us human beings to own who we are.

Introduction

The journey of every human, which starts from the womb through patience and persistence, does not happen overnight. It is like travelling to a foreign land; only when people disembark do they realize that they are at a place with its own language, customs, rituals, rubrics and taboos. Women are lifelong citizens of this land where motherhood is created to bring forth something which has never been crystallized through the "aeons". Sometimes, people around might not understand the journey because it is not for them. But in this journey, only women can hear what others cannot, have knowledge of what is mystified and stand the reflections.

In the course of this life journey, a woman named Rita understood how hard it would be, but knowing that every trial within the journey carries the potential for triumph, she focused on the destination with a smile on her face. She did not think of the failure but rather of the success that might come tomorrow, with an understanding that nature had set her on a difficult task and she could only succeed if she persevered. She was positively aware that it is not the eye that sees the beauty of the heavens, nor the ear that hears the sweetness of the music but the soul that perceives the relish of sensual and intellectual perfections, that would have greater perceptions of the events ahead.

In Africa, especially in Nigeria where Rita came from, she had witnessed the desperation and disorder of the powerless, and the treatment womenfolk receive from many cultural men – those who believe women are not created and should not be ranked as humans. Mariama Ba, in her book, *So Long a Letter,* had expressed critically how African womanhood is being viewed by some local culture-bound men who make the women surrender or adjust their stance and actions to suit theirs. This is done when the woman is forced to:

> Sacrifice all her possessions as gift to her families and in-laws. Beyond her possessions, she gives up her personality and dignity, to become just an ordinary thing in the service of the man who has married her. Everything about her and her behaviour is conditioned to suit everyone in her community.

Eva Figes laments in her book, *The Patriarchal Attitude,* that: 'Some women have lived down to the abysmally low standard.' These women, according to Figes, are presented with images in a mirror to be what womanhood is created for in this world. The 'women have to dance to the image in a hypnotic trance.' They are conditioned to the image they are shown in the mirror and they assume it to be what womanhood is. It is not only one mirror that is presented to these women, but 'the whole halls of mirrors which the male created.'

Liz Benson, the famous Nigerian actress, in her movie titled "Yesterday", depicts the pains of female circumcision, the agony of violent rapes and the grief of womanhood. She does not see the mournful image of womanhood as a sacrifice or a looking mirror, but rather as 'a victim of socio-cultural gang-up against mother Africa.'

Rita imagined how all these had twisted the lives of children who had been brought to the world; how narrow the path between humiliation and untrammelled fury is for these children and how easily African youths have slipped into violence and despair in many nations. She calculated the response to these disorders as inadequate for the task and sensed the intimate effort on her part as a woman. Rita knew that to understand this struggle would be to be placed at the centre of the crisis – Washington DC of the United States of America, a place where African residents have come to learn to respect womanhood.

She anticipated that the journey to this great city will aid gender equality in Africa and further help shape the lives of the children back home in Nigeria and in the diaspora for years to come. This idea moved Rita to sense the hardening of lines and the embrace of fundamentalism which had doomed all human beings in every culture. She knew there are serious discriminations against womanhood and children back home in Africa and elsewhere, and thought this would take more of perseverance than endeavour to tackle. The journey to the mainstream door of Washington DC would suit her and help integrate both gender as well as open a wider door for improvement. Rita believed many children and youths in Africa and the diaspora would benefit from her.

Rita compared the stories she had heard about men in the United States of America with some happenings in Africa, and thought the stories to be true. But when she got to the centre of this great country, she realized they were fabrications by some individuals who wanted to assume selfish leadership.

She later learnt that many African men in the United States value their women more than those in African-bound cultures, as they have witnessed and valued life from different perspectives. These men have come to know the power of gender equality and have given respect to it. They have realized how strong and wonderful motherhood is, as it is mandatory for them to be at the hospital with their women to witness the birth of their children and to value raising these children together, or end up in jail for not contributing to their welfare. Not in many parts of Africa does this happen as most men are not allowed into the hospital wards during the stage of bringing in new life, thus life is accorded minimal respect. Many men in the United States are sensitive to the entire aura and mystique of children and womanhood because the eye of the government, women organizations and equal right fighters are on everyone. These foreign men already know that every life is clothed in strength and dignity and both gender have to work together for the future of the next generation.

Rita also observed that in the United States, everyone is taught from childhood to realize and strive to be proud of oneself no matter the sex. Everyone strives to do well in spite of the losses and sorrows, as no one can choose the things that happens to one or who one is. Each person should be grateful for everything at all times. All human beings hold the empty bowls of life in their hands and have the capacity to fill them up. And a life falls apart when the foundation it is built on is not reliable, because God Almighty had lined up everything for each person. Therefore, the biggest adventure is to live the life of one's dream.

Rita had fought for womanhood and children in many areas in Africa, especially in Nigeria. It was during one of those fights for gender equality when she almost lost her life that brought her to the United States of America. She also decided to leave Nigeria because she believed that the impact she had made in her community would endure forever.

In the United States of America, Rita took the decision to undergo self discovery and she resolved to self-solitude in finishing the journey of womanhood. She saw every moment in life as an invitation to live out one's weakness or strength, notwithstanding whether one is a man or a woman. The opportunity for infinite possibilities exists for all.

Rita reached a point where the powers of her youth was gone; the possibility of failure presented itself and the dreams of earlier times in fighting for others seemed shallow and pointless. She found herself asking some tough questions: What could she do now while she was still here on this earth? What could she do with the life, gifts and opportunities given to her as a woman of integrity? Because the journey is natural and alive, she has to take advantage of each day. She is also aware that in this competitive world, God has made womanhood a reflection of His creativity, resourcefulness and imagination. What really matters would be that one is making real efforts to appreciate the gifts life has given to each of us.

Rita had ignored these questions because of the accompanying personal responsibilities and that of many others she had to consider. But all of a sudden, old truths and ideals no longer served her. She became restless, unhappy and full of an undefined ache. She was at a crossroads with no clear-cut idea of what path to follow because of several disappointments, but she knew she needed a change, and fate had brought her down to Washington DC in the United States of America to crown her with this honour. She was sure God divinely guides motherhood success for all mankind but she had to work hard to show this.

Rita noticed that many women and children back home in Africa inhibit their capacity for growth because the culture encourages them to live the life of uniformity. They stall, deny and ignore the ensuing crisis because of fear, confusion and a general malaise. Many go against the prevailing currents, step out of line, and break out with a polite society to follow unwritten rules of relationships.

So many quietly and obediently accept the abuses of power in the workplace, and blithely live with life's myriad of problems when they are destined to their own burgeoning desires. It would mean gradually letting go of that which was finished or outlived which would enable these women make room and welcome unlived possibilities. Every human being is born to be what one is created to be; to take responsibility for the space one holds, and to look back again and again and embrace that person everyone is intended to become. But many deny themselves this just as Simone de Beauvoir said: 'One is not born a woman; one becomes one.'

Reading a lot of books about what past generations of women had undergone and witnessing the ways of life of people in Africa had all fuelled Rita's imagination. From these, she had drawn conclusions which had become the catalyst for her motherhood logic and ideologies and had enabled her to take action. Rita had come to realise that all that mattered was to be able to satisfy the pinnacle and premier of motherhood.

Rita had come to learn from the Oprah Winfrey Show which she watched every day that 'we all are masters of our fate and captains of our soul, and there is nothing kept prepared for the journey.' Life whispers into every human being, and it is left to each to grasp whatever is whispered because 'we are more than what we were created to be.'

The primary responsibility of womanhood is to impact in the next generation the value of integrity. Motherhood is there to teach, support and assist each generation to become all it could be from the cradle. It is from the womb of motherhood that George Washington, James Madison, Benjamin Franklin, John Adam, Thomas Jefferson, Bill

Clinton, George Bush, Barack Obama, Hillary Clinton and a host of others with moral and mental capacity to draw up plans for the greatest country in the history of civilisation, all came forth. These men and women have continued to build and reshape the United States of America till date.

Great ancient and modern philosophers, psychologists, scientists and men and women that are geniuses in other fields, whom God created to be diviners and whom Plato had referred to as "noblest and gentlest" born to this world, are all from the iconic womb of womanhood. In life, people are created to become younger and wiser inwardly as they move from one stage to another while their physical body continues to change with age and environmental conditions.

Life continues to change like the ocean shore, constantly rearranging itself. The only trick is to welcome life and work with it positively and not against it. The fodder needed to continue this independent journey is knowing, acknowledging and celebrating the phases of all one has passed through and how one has risen, and respecting each person's determination. The goal of life is to come of age with purpose and energy rather than live out one's days in nothingness. This is the journey of womanhood – an affair that pulls open the woman's heart and womb.

The journey of womanhood has become complicated by the woman's changing sense of self and her place in society. Women work to create a new balance between the "male-dominated" world and the private enclave of childbearing. Acknowledging the unified nature of these two efforts without compromise offers a very personal perception of the woman coming to terms with herself, the motherhood.

A strong woman will have enough strength for the journey, and only one with a strong mind will know that the journey is where she should build a firm foundation with the bricks others throw at her. The brain has no organ of sex and there is neither a female heart nor liver; therefore when motherhood journeys, she must leave pieces of her life behind everywhere she goes. With brave wings she flies to her final destination, taking the decision not to live in the past but to move on in the present, looking upward to God Almighty who gives free air to all. Motherhood knows that when God's breath is sent out, it never goes back; rather, it benefits all that has life. Thus, the spirit of God influences everything that exists in the universe.

The woman finds joy particularly in the child she brings into the world as her contribution to the next generation. This makes the female gender very strong and amiable. These inspired Rita greatly and became the creed for her womanhood actions. It also made her flame to continue to burn brightly, as she took advantage of each day as if it were her last and shook her head always for a comeback as her life was getting a new beginning. She remembered Maria Von Trapp's *Sound of Music* which says:

> *Climb every mountain,*
> *Ford every stream,*
> *Follow every rainbow,*

'Till you find your dream.
A dream that will need
All the love you can give,
Every day of your life
For as long as you live.

This song gave Rita the push to get a special key to unlock her life, owning to the fact that she was a strong woman, with an irreplaceable gift and love for motherhood.

Chapter One

It was a bitter cold evening in November and Rita was happy to have run away from the troubles in Nigeria. She wrapped herself in a soft and warm comforter enjoying a cup of hot tea. While watching a nice movie and thinking about the fact that she would not have had time to do this in Nigeria, the telephone rang. It was her best friend Ngozi, a professor and a colleague at the university.

'So you are able to settle down over there in America without your business and the family?' the voice questioned.

'Why not? I need a time out my friend,' Rita slammed back at her.

Back home, Rita would have been juggling between thinking about the university students, her business centre, the family and several women and children who were suffering but were neither able to defend themselves nor give up. She would never have had time for herself, how much more watch a movie. Her whole life had been centred on trying to please others and getting the family together.

'Of course, I know you have forgotten all of us here in Nigeria, the professor said with a note of sarcasm.

'What are you talking about?' Rita inquired, as she needed to block everything about home from her memory for the first time ever and concentrate on enjoying the new freedom. The telephone line got disconnected when she wanted to talk more.

This was usual with calls from Nigeria. If you were lucky, you could have a full sentence of a conversation before hearing the long beeping which indicated that the line had been disconnected. Anyway, Rita was not in the mood to talk to anyone so she went back to sipping her tea, watching the nice movie and ruminating upon the journey of womanhood – a journey which starts from a woman's youthhood through old age; the carrying of babies and caring for these babies from childhood to adulthood as well as caring for the whole family. This makes an African woman feel she is destined to work very hard to meet the demands of husbands, in-laws, children, grandchildren and the extended family. Rita was happy to be away for a while to think about life and womanhood.

At a point, she had naively thought getting married would mean more freedom for a woman, but she later learnt that a woman's problem starts from the moment she understands the difference between male and female, especially in African families where the female child is being treated differently and regarded as a second class citizen among certain cultures unlike her male counterparts.

Rita relaxed and took her mind off the movie for a while to think about the sufferings back home, where most women do not have time to recharge. Everything was with a deadline, though never any personal deadline, but the improvised deadlines set by the woman's affair. She tried to justify all the imbalances with illusions about the good service a woman must provide for all in the family and the community. Still, most men do not regard what women do as anything. Women tend to forget that as human beings, they need to take out time to relax, care for themselves and prove who they are. Instead, they are immersed in taking care of others all through their lives. That is why women are being taken for granted especially in culture-bound societies. In these areas, men and women would leave very early in the morning for their different workplaces. When they return home in the evening, the man would sit and cross his legs in the living room watching the television or reading the newspapers, while the woman goes to the kitchen to prepare food for the family, organises the house and makes sure the children are well taken care of.

The woman cooks for the family, breastfeeds the baby and sets the meal for the man. The woman also has to make sure that every member of the family is taken care of, including the man. The man, after dinner, rushes out to the club to meet with friends and enjoy himself, while the woman stays home preparing for the next day's family activities. The next morning, both the man and the woman leave for their individual places of work, and the cycle continues with no time out for the woman.

Though in Rita's case she had urged and instructed other women to take out time for themselves, with four kids in the university and one in high school, she would always overload herself, taking more than she could handle. While in the office, she had to make calls to be sure the family was okay and the little ones at home were taken care of. Life became hectic mostly because of the efforts required to maintain both the façade and the ability to keep going without pausing to think. Her reaction was that she had given her forties and fifties to the naivety of the journey of womanhood.

Taking out time, she wandered into her past and discovered that she had missed out on a lot of things and taken others for granted, some of which had landed many women in the hospital with high blood pressure, heart disease and pains all over the body. In the course of this journey women need the re-evaluation of their lives from time to time.

William Shakespeare rightly said that 'an unexamined life is not worth living.' Women have continued to be jugglers, managing everything in a smooth even flow and balancing the gravity of the family and community in sync with dexterity. The women try to give each person in the family the push so that all could remain suspended and none falls out of sequence. In the church and community, the women have to also be at the forefront.

In Rita's case, she did not stop the push but simply transferred all her energy into achieving success and carving a niche for herself in life. Not knowing when to stop and analyse the calendar when the light turns red, as well as asking the question: "Who am I beyond the roles I play?" have gotten her into many troubles especially with the men in Nigeria and other culture-bound African societies.

Rita pictured herself standing in the university auditorium addressing students, young men and women, while they gazed at her with anxiety, as if an actress had inhabited her body, perfected her lines and happily taking the stage to deliver them. This companionship kept Rita going then. In running her business centre at the university, she organised everything and made sure that the following day's supplies were ordered and would be delivered on time. From the lecture room, she often rushed to the Coca Cola depot to arrange for the supply of drinks for the business centre. The home front was not left out. It must be taken care of as well. She went home very late and sat up all night preparing the following day's lectures. Thinking about all these reminded Rita that 'when at a crossroads, the heroine wants to make her own decisions whereas the weakling wants it made for her.'

Rita had decided to go to the United States to gather the threads of her experiences and recycle them into a newer and more colourful tapestry, even though she did not really know what it was she was supposed to do next. Therefore, to understand her mission, she must depart from the mundane to refine her spirit and listen to life's whispers. She hesitated for a while on these thoughts and whispered: 'Why not, it is high time you did something spontaneous for yourself, Rita'. Relieved, she went back to the nice movie she was watching. The theme of the movie reminded her that the law of womanhood determines how one manages the moment, move into position and strategically adapt and forge ahead without fear. The wisdom would enable the woman know herself as a woman of integrity and know when to slow down, step back, accelerate, cringe, capture and step up.

Rita has come to realise that the art of being a woman is getting the inside vision to materialise on the outside, and that the innovative visions of womanhood can only give her a voice if transformed into a mosaic masterpiece through self-examination. She has figured out that people can either be true or not, depending on their frame of mind. Besides, each person must make little adjustments in life, which won't require complete rethinking.

These thoughts energised Rita and got her out of bed. She re-dialled the number of her professor friend, but could not reach her. She heard a recorded female voice say, 'The number you have dialled is switched off.' She dialled again and the same female voice said, 'You are not authorised to dial this number. Please check the number and dial again.' She made another attempt and the same female voice said, 'The number you dialled does not exist.' Rita was sure she had dialled the right number, but didn't care because this was the normal problem with Nigerian network providers.

She tried to forget about Nigeria's telephone problems and began asking herself questions, which she already knew the answers to. It was the fear factor, the same fear that had crippled many ridiculous culture-bound people, especially in Africa and many other parts of the world, making some women mere "housewives", and men "house bands" instead of heads of families. It is okay to be fearful but never allow fear keep you from becoming who you ought to be. As Joyce Meyer had said, 'Feel the fear and do it anyway.' God created fear in all as a tool to teach human beings to be cautious, compassionate and calculating. But when fear is refined by experience, it becomes a tool for survival.

Rita believed marriage is supposed to be a division of labour where the man and woman have a fair share of responsibilities – the man, masculine and powerful in strength, with the woman, feminine, witty and powerful in wisdom – both working and merging to make a better combination. This is how nature had designed it to be; gender equality, where no one wins or loses.

Chapter Two

The decision to leave Nigeria was not an easy one for Rita to make. She finally made up her mind after she came to realise that many of the women she was fighting for had decided to turn against her. These women had been indoctrinated by culture and were afraid that their lives would always hang on the men. Many of the things the women would have done without the sanction of the men would be seen as abomination. Most women in Africa believe these notions and live with them.

Rita had given several lectures on gender equality in the universities and many other places, to help people understand the essence of gender equality and each person's right as a human being and the fact that everyone's life is a miracle of chance waiting for its destiny to be shaped and there is nothing that can be so easily remade as the definition of our selves. Many of the bottlenecks women in many cultures experience have to do with relationships with the family. It is important for everyone to define who he/she is, or else such a person will be crunched into other people's fantasies and be swallowed up.

Rita believes that embracing womanhood can make every woman bold, courageous and imaginative; exactly what the patriarchal culture fears and has often tried as much as possible to subdue, control and even use to traumatise the female gender with fear. If a woman understands her powers, she would have access to the energy and insight that would make her feel connected to a higher purpose in all areas of life. Women have the combination of potential, muse and energy and a powerhouse of confidence. But the fear of the patriarchal world that the female might supersede them in the family and elsewhere has given rise to the flexing of muscles to intimidate the matriarchal, thereby exposing men's chauvinistic actions especially in Africa.

When men started waging war against themselves in Rita's town in Nigeria, she decided to call for a private meeting with the women to decide, as a group, on disassociating themselves from the men's local politics. In that meeting, all the women took an oath and promised not to join the men in their war but to stick together in peace, for the sake of their children and the future generation.

'We have to stand by each other no matter what,' the women resolved, and took the decision at the end of the meeting not to join the men in their war which all believed would lead the entire town and future generation to destruction.

To Rita's surprise, she found out that many of the women had become their own worst enemies, dogged by fear of perfectionism, guilt and the need to perform. The family, intricate as a spider web draped over numerous limbs, has hundreds of pine cones underneath its women.

Many branches of the family are entrusted to the women and these enslave them to the men as a majority of these women cannot think outside the men's direction. With the spouses, children, in-laws and extended relations of the family, the web is complicated. The decision is to keep a firm hold of womanhood by showering everyone with love through peaceful solutions. But what Rita saw were women being brainwashed not to believe in womanhood; rather, to cling to the men to be able to keep the home fire burning. All these ill-doings took their toll on women and showed the women's greatest epiphany during her years and made many of them to become incomplete as they wade through the tides of events.

Rita's experience with these women had taught her that those committed to conformity are comfortable at a particular level in life. They may feel threatened if one tries to open a wider door. But it would require a very strong-willed woman of integrity to venture out on her own and stand firmly for the truth. Out of fear, many women turn against themselves criticizing and sabotaging the group's efforts. But these criticisms will never impede any progress if one stands firm as a strong woman in honesty and truthfulness.

The women of Rita's town were to have the fiftieth anniversary of their coming together as a union. They had started this union from the early 1940s and were able to establish so many edifices in the town. The only girls secondary school in her hometown was built by the women. The same is true of the Women Primary School.

When there was an incident of schools' closure in the whole state due to non-payment of teachers' salaries, the women decided to start a private elementary school on their own to keep the children of the town out of trouble. They employed qualified teachers and began running the school till date.

The women also built the only maternity hospital in the town, the health care centre and a multi-purpose centre where women are trained in crafts and other entrepreneurial skills. The women happened to be the backbone of all the churches. Without these women, 'most obsequies would be a farce, without decency and the joy of life would be denied all men in the town', stressed Chief V.A. Obi in 2010. These women were planning to celebrate these achievements and show how strong womanhood had been in their town. As quoted by this respectable chief of the town earlier mentioned, 'When men quarrelled over irrelevant matters in a drinking bar, women in their calmer perspective saw things in a different way and used their persuasive attributes to settle them.'

During this period, Rita was entrusted with a huge sum of money by the women to prepare souvenirs and make other plans for the occasion. Some men at this point decided to pick an unfounded quarrel with the women, a way to show that no matter what happens in their culture-bound areas in Nigeria, men should be in charge of all affairs. It was a personality issue which the men wanted the women to be involved in. Some men from Rita's village and other villages began framing up lies against the traditional leader, his cabinet and some of the men who supported the women.

The town was made up of nine villages, and some men from four of the villages, one of which happened to be Rita's village, started the problem. But Rita maintained that women must be neutral and should not join the men in the fight.

During one of the meetings, one of the women challenged Rita, stating that men have every right over the women and children. Therefore, women have no right to disobey their husbands and they must stand by them notwithstanding their being right or wrong. Thus, she was questioning the women's authority to disobey their husbands. To Rita's greatest surprise and that of womanhood, a majority of the women agreed with the speaker's opinion. Rita tried to prove them wrong but failed because they had been indoctrinated by the men. Many of the women were fearful of what would happen if they told the truth.

With these women's mentality at this point, Rita's vanity began to outrun her sanity. She decided to keep quiet and listen to their arguments. At a point, the concert of sounds made while these women argued and their reasoning engulfed Rita. When she could not entertain their reasoning anymore, she quietly reminded them: 'We are talking of what is right for the entire town and village, most especially the children who are our future generation, and not only the present men and women.' Rita could not believe her ears what these women were saying against the decisions they had earlier taken. She asked the women to give her cogent reasons why they should stand with the men in their quarrel and a lady from the crowd answered: 'Because they are men and they know better than the women, and most importantly "men" own all the women.'

Rita noticed that these women had been conditioned and committed to conformity as they felt threatened to voice the truth. Many kept quiet for fear of being noticed. That was the same fear the men had instilled in womanhood.

The women had been socialised to believe that they were just like little children and needed to be guided by the men. According to the stories told to them, life for every woman undergoes a constant metamorphosis and it needs to be guided by men and nature, thus the need for the payment of the bride price on every woman in their culture. But the bride price is just a cultural ceremony which will neither make one static nor debase one from being what God has created one to be.

To the men, the changing powers of a woman's body suggest that women go through different phases from time to time. These phases affect the women emotionally, spiritually, physically and physiologically. That is why they think they have to be around to guide, direct and protect women all through their lives. Rita wondered why men talk about the changes in every woman's body, which is natural, making it seem as if it was a downside to be a woman.

The first seven years of a woman are filled with wonders and development. From seven to fourteen, women are hormonal; from fourteen to twenty-one, they become sexual; from twenty-one to twenty-eight, they experience the desire to procreate, after which their time is consumed with mothering and putting others first. At thirty-five, women begin to look beyond a limited existence; between forty-two and forty-five, menopause sets in, after which, with greying hairs the woman becomes "a watchdog".

According to the men, all through these stages, men are constant in their lives, strong and energetic. This is a belief which is instilled in these women.

These stages of life for women are natural and make the woman strong and wise, as she gains knowledge and wisdom from the time spent going through them. But the women tend to forget that the men undergo their own stages of transformation as human beings too.

The men had convinced all women to pull out of the women's association, which is the umbrella body of the women's wing, and be on their side, while they fought for an "autonomous town" in the community. They called for a joint meeting of all men and women. In the meeting, all the women and some of the men who supported the women agreed to stand with the men and fight for the "autonomous community" and against the traditional leader. Rita was left on her own and was also mandated by the men to produce the money given to her by the town women for the fiftieth anniversary preparation.

Meanwhile, they had also decided to start their own "autonomous women's" meeting.

The meeting took place at about twelve midnight. As the meeting was going on, Rita's mind searched for many answers. She watched as the women smiled and jubilated with the advice they were getting from the men. Gazing up into the sky, she saw the moon and stars slipping out of sight, their glow only visible along the rim of high clouds. Anger, as an injection, flooded her body and mind but she could not use hatred to ease the pain, rather she had to bear it.

Rita stopped listening to whatever they were saying at a certain point and came to realise how wrapped-up she had been in her own perceived injuries as she continued staring at the moonlight. She could see many stars moving very fast, some shooting stars disappearing, and was also able to see the image in the full moon as she concentrated on the work of nature. Rita became eager to escape the imaginary traps that humanity had set for womanhood. To the men's world, she was willing to surrender the values of her life, as if those values were somehow irreversibly soiled by the endless falsehoods these men had spoken. She began to build survival strategies under stress and knew immediately that her motherhood journey will depend on the choice she was about to make at that point and it would affect every aspect of her life. Subconsciously, she felt empty of ideas but took a bold decision on what to do next.

Rita sat with the women but was deep in thought, and asked herself how this had happened? Then she said quietly to herself, 'You cannot lose the fight Rita. Your introspection, as a woman of integrity and womanhood, which is about who you are and who you might become, should not grow stunted and narrow.' The fear was that she believed she did not belong with them. She whispered to herself, 'Rita, unless you hide and pretend to be something you aren't, you will forever remain an outsider.'

The faces of the women in the room reminded Rita of the young and ignorant youths and a quote from Maya Angelou's book, *I Know why the Caged Bird Sings*:

> Most surrender to vague and murderous pressure of adult conformity. It becomes easier to die and avoid conflicts than to maintain a constant battle with the superior forces of maturity.

Rita realised that most of the women were afraid and unhappy with the situation, but it would not be easy for them to take the punishment meted out by the men. She felt the command to grow up and defend motherhood would be more bearable than the faceless horror of wavering purpose, which these women had surrendered to; and she reasoned that the motherhood gifts should inspire women to look beyond the usual to identify the unusual. Rita immediately remembered what Emily Dickinson once said: 'If one's nerves denies anyone, the person should better go above those nerves.' She also remembered Maya Angelou's saying: 'Without courage one cannot practice any virtue with consistency.' With this in mind, Rita decided to take a drastic step, knowing that time is a wonderful storyteller.

Rita began to imagine the faces of other women she had read in history who had fought for their freedom and rights and wondered what these women would say to her if they were here. She remembered the face of the late Susan Anthony who fought for women's right to vote in America but died before the 19th amendment was constituted into the United States Constitution which is now being remembered by all. The late Fumilayo Ransome Kuti, the Nigerian lady, who inspired and energised womanhood in Africa with her actions to fight for the rights of women. The faces of other women like Rosa Park, Flora Nwapa, Elizabeth Adekogbe, Nawal El Saadawi, Sheeba Aslam Fehmi, Eva Cox, Victoria Gray Adams, Mary Ruwart, Molara Ogundipe, Diane Nash, Marian Wright Edelman, Myrlie Evers Williams, and many more who had fought for civil rights and womanhood, all staring at her and expecting her to react for the future generation. She realised that what bound her and those women together in the meeting went beyond anger or despair or pity.

What are these famous women who had fought for womanhood asking of her now? Rita thought. Determination; the determination to push against whatever power that will make her stoop instead of standing straight. The determination to resist the easy and expedient way. She then called her name several times as she usually does when she is faced with an unimaginable circumstance and said, 'Rita, you might be locked into a world not of your own making, but you still have a claim on how it is shaped.'

Rita knew that she still had responsibilities and she decided that her identity and responsibility would be what she would choose to believe. Despite what people might say, she must refuse to compromise her high standards, for she 'belongs to a community of humans that anchors on truth and cannot be swayed by worldly opinion,' she said silently. 'No matter what happens, I must focus on the truth, and stand strong with confidence knowing that all will be well.'

Rita thought that at her age and status in life, she should be aiming for "the gold of motherhood". Moreover, she had learnt that being true to oneself and letting one's personality shine through are essential virtues in life. If Rita must be herself, then she has to automatically stand out in the crowd, because there is no one like her in the entire world. She will have to show her people that she is equal to her pride and greater than her pretensions.

She left the meeting and swore to attend the women's anniversary ceremony all by herself from her village and damn the consequences. First of all, she told her family of her intentions and implored her husband not to get involved whenever the men were having any gathering against the women. Her husband did not take it kindly though. He knew his wife very well and realized how far she could go to fight for the rights of women and children. Rita thought of all she had single-handedly changed for the sake of womanhood in her village and town and resolved to add her intended achievement to the list.

At the time she got married to her husband, her father-in-law, a traditional man, had schooled her on how the women were regarded in their village. 'There are so many things women are not supposed to have privilege to according to culture,' he had warned her. 'Women have to answer "sir" and "yes sir" to their husbands always. She could be punished for doing anything the man deemed to be wrongful in the family. She cannot eat eggs because it is a symbol of childbirth. If any egg is cooked in the family, the girls, women and children are not allowed to eat it, only the men are allowed to eat eggs; for this symbolises the woman eating her own child. The way chickens lay eggs is the same way women give birth to their children,' her father-in-law had stressed. 'Therefore, it would be an abomination for any woman to eat an egg at any time of her life,' the father-in-law had re-emphasised. She was also told that allowing children to eat eggs would mean leading them to steal later in life.

There are also parts of a chicken and meat women were not supposed to eat. Women couldn't eat gizzard, the heart of a chicken, or the heart of other kinds of animals, as these parts were meant for the men. The man owns most of the delicious parts of any meat while the woman owns the other parts, most of which were bones. That's why the women are called '*Ada neli ukwu anu*', in Igbo culture, which means that daughters are privileged to the lower parts of all meat, which were mostly of bones.

Rita could not believe her ears when she heard all these. That was being extremely selfish on the part of the men and culture. She asked her father in-law if the woman would die if she ate any of those forbidden parts of the meat. His answer was that such a woman would be punished and banished from the village.

As Rita did not come from a family that observed all these, she made it clear to her husband's family that she was not going to observe any of those established norms and she never did.

She told them that in her family, both boys and girls, men and women have equal rights to all parts of any meat, including unrestricted eating of eggs, and this she brought into her marriage. Because of her behaviour and attitude, a lot of people in her husband's town regarded her as an "outcast". She made it clear to her father-in-law and all the men that she came from a family that does not observe all those rules and she was not ready to change because she got married into their family. They tried everything to make her live by their rules but failed. Finally, her husband was left with no choice than to support her.

The night before the fiftieth anniversary of the women group, a special emissary was sent to Rita's house to warn her of the consequences if any woman should defy the men's authority. 'The woman should not come back to the village but should go straight to her father's house, never to come back to her husband,' the men warned. The famous town crier came specially to tell Rita what the men had decided and stressed the fact that 'No woman from their village should attend the meeting.'

Rita asked why and the answer she was given was that 'the men were in control.' Her next question was: 'Since when have the women and men of this village been having such gatherings or meetings?' The town crier could not answer the question. Rita then told the town crier that because he had no answer to her questions, she would attend the women's anniversary meeting, and that he should go back and tell the men that she has resolved to stand with other women in the community.

The following morning, the trucks were loaded with the souvenirs for the "Town Women at Fifty" from Rita's house and driven to the meeting hall. Many people from her village came out to see if she would defy the men's orders. Men and women stood along the road to see if Rita would attend the meeting. Her husband fearing what might happen, left for the city that day because he knew how far the wife would go to fight for womanhood and the next generation.

Rita made sure her children were in the car with her and her first son was at the wheels as they headed to the meeting venue. An entourage of some women from nearby villages as well as law enforcement officers escorted her from her house to the meeting hall, with the women's flag flying behind them. Rita was completely filled with happiness, and the best way she could describe the situation of things at that moment was 'Awesome, wonderful, marvellous and adorable for womanhood.' When she got to the meeting venue, tears of joy like dews from heaven flowed down from her eyes uncontrollably.

As she entered the hall, she was hailed with songs and praise. This made her proud of herself and the journey of womanhood and it became a defining moment in her life. She sat down at the high table with other women of integrity and "the moment froze", as if caught on a daguerreotype, and the minutes that followed moved like that of 'a slow montage' as Maya Angelou would describe it. In her inner mind, Rita believed one should not fear change, rather one should embrace it. She believed that a person who does not know what he/she wants in life, has no chance of getting anything out of it.

Rita became consumed with the thought of Rosa Park, Martin Luther King Junior and many other people who had fought for human rights and succeeded. She did not care what the outcome would be. At that moment, she was happy she had made a mark on history in her town and defended womanhood.

Recalling and taking stock of the past years while listing all the events and moments, Rita identified this particular moment as exhilarating. At that moment, she thought she had done better. A decade has made such a difference. "What has transpired? Who was she back then? What had she actually accomplished? What has been left undone?" Perhaps answering these questions would give her a glimpse of the unfolding plot. She felt it was a waste of time to dwell on the past, recalling these key moments and in so doing realising that nothing that had happened was commonplace, as 'change can either come slowly or hit like a thunder storm or a hurricane'.

Aside from looking in the mirror at emerging days and white hairlines on her forehead, 'it was difficult to identify the moment of actual metamorphosis as the men did compared to the women', Rita thought. For every human being changes subtly, and all do change at different stages of life. This reminded Rita of William Shakespeare's poem on the stages of man, which says:

> All the world's a stage,
> And all men and women are merely players;
> They have their exits and their entrances,
> And one man in his time plays many parts ...
> (William Shakespeare – *The Seven Stages of Man*).

Rita believed that these stages apply to all humans. The strength she regained by making her own decisions gave womanhood hope. The joy of her autonomy and the resurgence of will was worth it. And she no longer felt confused because she had unintentionally become a change agent – a woman willing to share her experiences in order to help other women find themselves. From that moment, Rita felt she had created an identity for herself and from there came an immediate feeling of being true to herself. This gave her strength of fidelity.

That night, all the women leaders from her village had stormed Rita's house to question her reasons for defying the men's orders, but she boldly ordered them out. After that incident, she was no longer harrassed by the men from her village. One thing she gained was the respect of her children, and more importantly, that of her husband. He loved her more, not the adolescent kind of love she faintly remembered when they first got married, but something deeper and more unconditional. This she found out when she got a visa to travel to the United States of America, and her husband gave her a present on which he scribbled, 'the lady of integrity', and urged her to be strong and be herself and not pretend to be who or what she was not, for he will always trust her actions anywhere in the world.

The traditional ruler of her town and other respectable personalities and the entire state respected her actions. The following year, a lot of women joined the women group. These women became as bold as Rita and questioned the "men's autonomous community" just as Rita had done. Rita decided that 'instead of living one's life stagnantly, one should choose to be more actively involved in other people's life. It made Rita believe that her courage in the faith that her eternal resilience has given her joy and hope as this comes back to each human created spontaneity.

This reminded Rita that adults are always eager to applaud their children's accomplishments such as walking, climbing, jumping, running and speaking, but they hardly notice their own. People may not change so much outwardly as growing children do, but they are evolving internally all the time. Every decade brings with it a new certainty, a time of passage and stage in life as observed by William Shakespeare. Rita believed it would be interesting if there were actual rituals at the end of each decade to mark one's achievements and managed crises, affirming life's progress. Throughout her life, Rita had learnt that old species leave, new ones arrive, but the processes of creation and change remain.

Change won't come ordinarily; it must start somewhere. Communities have to be created, fought for and tended to like gardens. They expand or contract with people's dreams; and through organising and shared sacrifice, their membership is earned. She believes that change in their cultural society, where womanhood would be recognised, will be the uniqueness of her own life.

Before she left Nigeria for the US, the men questioned her on why she had defied their authority. Many of them were very angry with her. They expressed their anger that she disgraced them before the whole community, because she happened to be the only woman from the four villages who set the pace of defying the men's authority. Her candid answer was that no one gave her the actual reason why she should not attend the meeting being organised by the town women. Moreover, men and women, for over fifty years, have always had separate meetings, Women's Patriotic Union and Men's Patriotic Union. The men do not have any authority in the women's union, but they all work together for the good of the future generation.

The women themselves were secretly happy for her but they were not brave enough to act as she did. Some of them later visited her house very late in the night when all had gone to sleep to applaud her bravery. They must not be seen by anyone or else they would be punished.

With time, many women from the villages got influenced by Rita's actions. They began to openly defend womanhood, refusing to live silently as second class citizens. The men began planning Rita's kidnap. She was secretly warned to leave the country and was able to obtain a visa to travel to the United States of America for good.

Chapter Three

Rita left for the United States of America to start a new life. The first time she was there, she had come in as a student with her husband and they returned to Nigeria immediately after she finished her first master's degree in Education.

Before she left for the the US this second time, a friend of hers visited her house in the village and made a comment about Rita's family house that got to her. 'This house, I suppose, has outlived its usefulness, hasn't it?' Rita's friend said. It was a family house in which they had raised their five children. Four of them were then in the university and seldom came home for holidays. Rita and her family did not travel to the village to visit with other extended family members like they used to. And so they needed a house of their own, not the family house that was built years back. Rita and her husband had decided that it was time for them to have their own privacy; a place where the children and their grandchildren would call their own. They immediately started the building project and completed it in record time. They moved out of the family house to the new one and during the weekends, they travelled home together for visits.

Their children were adults and could decide to travel to other places on their own to visit their friends during the holidays. Rita felt it was worth it to have a place where they could come back to when they felt like.

Rita and her husband had a lifetime full of memories attached to the old family town house, but it was time for them to move on, to start a new life in another home. When the house was finished, some sections were rented out to keep the compound warm. The family, with time, learnt that 'reflecting on what is outlived in one's life today ruins it; as does clinging to old ways, outdated ideals and a lifestyle that has run its course.' Perhaps one of the reasons she felt so compelled to move to the US was to have a change of environment. Motherhood allows one to adapt to change and grow stronger. Change is sometimes very painful to endure but it helps people to discover and embrace what is inside of them and keeps them moving forward.

No one can control the way life passes; people can only adapt. Rita believes that by merely taking the decision to move on, there is always something bigger, better and more life-giving to be found. The journey is not only about progressing through the world but also moving through stages of understanding. Each experience in life is an opportunity to learn, grow and discover that which is within; to bloom with gratitude at countless opportunities and express oneself more fully and completely.

In the plane to the United States of America, Rita sat by the window and watched the cloud as it floated by. She could not help but think about her mother. She used to be a very pretty and vibrant lady but is now worn and tired due to old age. 'The most beautiful flower must one day sag, fade and change colour while new ones bloom more beautiful than ever,' she mused to herself.

As the plane moved further into the cloud, Rita felt as though she and her mother were flying in the air like birds. Trying to hold on to her old and fragile mother as well as keep both afloat ran her out of energy. Rita at the moment only had the strength to fly to safety on her own as she was still strong and energetic, but her mother was not. If she went under, both of them would.

The choice was obvious, although enormously very painful. Rita could never leave her mother alone, but she knew she was entitled to a life that would not always include her. The older one gets, the stronger the wind for 'every age has a keyhole to which its eye is passed.' This is the only fee God charges for life. She realised that it was impossible to regenerate the mother's mind, will, determination, agility and her release from old age which she was experiencing at that moment. So she had to fly at her own pace and leave her mother to complete her life's journey all by herself. All Rita could do would be to render a little help that would not be detrimental to both of them. Each person is to journey gracefully to her own destiny.

It is funny how time changes the human perspective. When she was a little girl, the happiness of her life seemed a natural thing, as inevitable as the coming season. Rita took life for granted, never questioning what was placed before her. What she didn't know then was that elderly people shoulder tremendous burden both financially, emotionally and physically so that even the strongest of human begins to break down with time and she was no exception. Now, Rita's mother is gone and is only remembered by the relics and footprints she had left behind.

One day, as she walked on the street, she picked some inviting pieces of wood she saw on the ground and the thought that the pieces were once parts of a whole flashed across her mind. Now they were cracked and broken; time had softened the edges and made each a new one all on its own. This represented a nice metaphor for someone who had evolved through the passages of personality.

Sometimes, it is very phoney to relax and try to understand what life is all about and not be prepared for the journey. Life is an undeniable miracle. When one knows better, one will do better. One must never try to please anybody but oneself. It is also important to learn from every experience and grow to greatness, and at the same time be at peace with oneself and celebrate every age one had lived.

At one time, many have fallen and every man and woman have made mistakes. Just as our Lord Jesus said to the people, 'He that is without sin among you should be the first to cast a stone' (John 8: 7), when the people brought to Him the woman whom they were about to stone to death for committing adultery. As a matter of fact, no one should be put down based on what people say about them. Rita had learnt never to be discouraged or cry over the mistakes she had made as a young girl. Instead, she had tried to learn from every of those mistakes, allowing the experience to guide her on the journey.

Rita compared life to a woman who spends years holding her family members together, becoming unhinged when they are gone and no longer need to be attached to each other. She remembered her little children and grandchildren who were very close to their mother and grandmother. Now they are all grown and need to live for themselves. Sometimes she desires to cuddle and sleep with them just as she did when they were little, but to them it is odd. The children now need their independence and their peers to play and discuss with. This means there will always be a generation gap and each generation needs space to grow.

Another time, Rita was directed to a toenail stone wilting in the dry sand, clinging to another. She was struck by the stench that came from such clinging, holding on when it might have been better to let go. It reminded her of how many people she has clung to or allowed to cling to her as a mother, long after it ceased to be a healthy thing to do. 'Wisdom can come from unwise places,' she told herself. Every life's journey has a story and one has to take responsibility for the space one occupies.

As Rita pictured her mothers' life and hers, she remembered her own children. They were grown and should have their own lives to live. She cannot cling to them forever. Now that she was getting older, she cannot pull them backwards. Sometimes, motherhood forgets that children are grown and need their own space.

Rita resolved to move on, with this heaviness in her heart, to the United States of America, far from home. On getting to the States and meeting other youths, she was reminded of her own children, who seem perfectly happy with their distance from home. The sense that this made was that the children would relish their independence and their ability to reach out to their father and her only when they pleased.

In America, when Rita was able to appreciate solitude and independence, she was able to say 'So be it.' Would she have desired to raise "morons" as children who will have no interest in flying the coop? Even mother eagle pushes her young eaglet out from the nest when it realises it is time for the little bird to be on its own. At the initial stage, it may be hard for the young eaglet, but with time, it comes to discover how amazing its wings are. At that time, the eaglet will not need its mother anymore, but will start its own life, flapping its wings to greater, amazing and thrilling heights of new opportunities. At this time, it had come to understand that the nest was just temporary.

Mothers should be proud of their children and their thirst to chart the course of their own lives, but it is often not easy to let go of them. When she urges them forward, she does not want them to settle halfway across the country as she believes that the sky should be their limit. Just like the little eaglet, the world will open its doors to these children and they will learn that life's journey is full of joyful exuberance and it never ends. They will learn that there are lean times in the journey when they may fall but they must also learn that it is important never to remain where they have fallen but to get up and keep going, making the best of every situation to declare what they are created to be.

One thing Rita had learnt is that a mother can never outgrow her love for her children whether grown up or not. Yet, the intimacy she once shared, over time becomes nothing more than simply hope for loved strangers. One of Rita's friends had once told her that: 'Raising a child is the only relationship where, if you do it right, it ends up in separation,' and this is right because when one is thinking and worrying for the grown child, that child will be thinking and worrying about his or her loved ones somewhere in the universe. An Igbo adage says, '*Ana echelu nwa, Ona echelu onye di ya nma.*'

Relatively speaking, there is only a little time for mothering in this world, although it seems an all-consuming phase. The nuturing phase appears to stretch on forever, but in truth, it lasts only for few years, and then it's gone. Many of the big events of life are monumental, yet brief, unlike the first day a child is born which remains a vibrant memory; in truth, it is just a fleeting moment.

Once again, recognising that that which is outlived is the answer, Rita tried to stop thinking about life. This helped her to accept the constant reconfiguration of family just as observing the reconfiguration of her stay in the United States of America.

Being in the United States is like getting to a mountain top. There are moments when the soul takes wings. She started to think that she had passed through life's earlier stages and as such had much to offer and it was high time she honoured herself. She remembered she never thought to celebrate her life, and particularly not her body, not even once; neither after the birth of her children, nursing them through their young lives, nor the hundreds of times her arms had extended to console other children.

This brought to Rita's memory a time when her first son was about to get into the university and the family had no money. She took all her valuable jewellery and ornaments to a prominent lady friend from her town in Nigeria, who happened to know those who could buy them to enable her pay for her son's tuition fee. The lady, being a good friend to Rita, refused to collect the jewellery. She advised Rita to go home and sleep over the decision, knowing how African women valued these precious ornaments, but Rita maintained that her son had to get into the university immediately and there was no going back on the decision. So all her gold jewellery and other valuable ornaments were sold to a goldsmith at a reduced price to make sure the son got an education.

This trend of selling her precious things for the sake of her children's education continued with other children until Rita was able to start a small business to augment the little salary she was earning. Rita had always put her family and others first in her life, not taking care of herself. She desired that her children and others get what was denied her during her childhood. She did everything humanly possible to put her children first, even when it involved sacrificing her life.

Rita had been very focused, pushing onward and upward to goals set often by other people, against whom she measured herself. She recollected many atimes when she would be in a bad mood and people would asked her what ailed her. She did not have the answer because she neither chose to decipher the question, nor sat down to think about her life and what she was doing to herself especially after she lost her husband. With all these experiences, Rita came to know what was missing in her life. What she craved to have back was an integration of her feminine aspects. She desired a sense of balance that began in her core.

In America, she observed that many people reverence the stages and ages of human life as much as the passage of the seasons. Many do not denigrate a woman's ageing process but exalt it and see the experience as sacred, hence they do not care about her age in marriage or love affair. A woman can still get married to a younger person at the age of seventy, even to a man thirty years younger, which cannot happen in Africa.

Rita was happy that her children never forgot how she suffered for them. The children regarded her and treated her like a very precious ornament. During one surprise birthday party organised for her by her children, she was gifted a brand new vehicle. They provided everything humanly possible to keep her happy. She became her children's priority.

On a particular day, Rita went into a Christian bookstore in Manassas, Virginia and her eyes fell on a nice piece of crucifix. As she examined it, the first thought that came to her mind was the cross of Jesus Christ, while the second thought was direction, with the shape of the cross showing North, South, East and West. What about the centre of the cross? She began to think of God the creator of the universe, sitting at the centre of the universe, directing everything happening in the world and holding everything together. Jesus was placed at the centre when he was crucified with two other men, the two thieves, one on each side. This shows that the centre is very important in life.

To Rita, women are like crosses of various sizes and shapes. Some are absolutely plain, others with intricate designs but all bear the centre circle that appears to be the stabilising element that adds strength to four appendages. The cross, like womanhood, is where all the opposites come together in the family, the flow of humanity and a powerhouse with actions and reactions in life. Rita loved crosses for religious connotations but as she looked at that particular cross and its shape, she extended it to motherhood and its journey.

She imagined the north of the cross could bring "healing", the south "clarity in life", the west could offer "patience" and the east could be for "grace". Whatever she did in America, she bore the signs of the cross in her mind because she thought it would help her gain life and move on knowing that the Heavenly Father created womanhood like a cross, to bring forth new life into the world as well as hold the family together.

Rita began making friends, mixing up and reading biographies of other women – white, black, Jews, Latinos and Indians – who had made it, from Africa to different parts of the world, so as to know more about womanhood. Some of these women are Maya Angelou, Nancy Pelosi, Hillary Clinton, Professor Obioma Nnaemeka, Cicely Tyson, Oprah Winfrey, Michelle Obama, Angela Merkel, Janet Yellen, Harriet Tubman, Lucy Stone, Indira Gandhi, Kamla Persad-Bissessar, Peng Liyuan and many more. Imagining the faces of these women, Rita could see the familiarity of womanhood and thus came to the understanding that no one could make her feel inferior without her consent. These women exposed her to openness, frankness and kindness in their ritualistic walk for survival. The wisdom Rita got from reading about these women and the sense of familiarity gained, provided her with more energy as she travelled round America. This explains why Rita longed for those elusive qualities of womanhood, and it moved her to another level of the journey. These include the quality of authenticity; of being who one is; of possessing a truthfulness that goes beyond words; the encouragement to move forward; and a modest commitment to pull womanhood into the mainstream of events within a generation. This made the motherhood journey meaningful. Rita came to realise what the past and present generations of women had to overcome in their different cultures and she became optimistic of the ability of the next generation to continue advancing into the mainstream. These gave her the assurance that African culture will also advance in gender equality.

Rita sought healing to restore the soundness of mind and spiritual wholeness given to her because she had been open, very receptive and patient in the journey. She was also granted the greatest gift of all, the gift of clarity and contentment with all she had in the United States of America. She found herself laughing at the foolishness that in Africa one can shortcut one's way to get whatever one wants. But in the United States of America, nothing worthwhile can be achieved hurriedly and she had to learn this in a very hard way. Neither the season, the birth of a new life, death, the dawning of a new day, the setting of the sun, a thought, a work of art, any form of story, nor a written book can make that happen. Being patient and living life moment to moment can make experience meaningful, while not pretending to be someone else is what makes life well lived. So what is lasting is focusing on oneself and being truthful. Rita came to learn that whatever one does in the United States of America, "Big Uncle Sam" (the government) watches from all angles.

Still holding the cross in her hand and reflecting on many facets of womanhood, it reminded Rita, once again, of the woman who holds the family together. She thought of the most enduring part, the miracle of the changing body and its glorious attributes. What huamnaity failed to take into account in African culture is the neglect women have endured, no thanks to some men, and the fact that motherhood has submitted its bills several times but many of these men had paid no attention. Only the children did, but most of them join the culture immediately they become adult men.

She also came to realise that in life, sometimes, the journey could take a different direction which might be very difficult to comprehend and the sweetness of the journey could become sour. This made Rita remember the famous poem, *Invictus*, by William Ernest Henley:

> Out of the night that covers me
> Black as the Pit from pole to pole,
> I thank whatever gods may be,
> For the unconquerable soul.
>
> In the fell clutch of circumstance,
> I have not winced nor cried aloud.
> Under the bludgeoning's of chance,
> My head is bloody, but unbowed.
>
> Beyond this place of wrath and tears,
> Looms but the Horror of the shade,
> And yet the menace of the years finds,
> And shall find, me unafraid.

Rita paused to ponder on the poem and then she began to say aloud the last verse of the poem: 'It matters not how straight the gate, how charged with punishments the scroll, I am the master of my fate: I am the captain of my soul.'

She went to bed reciting the poem even in her dreams.

When her lower spine, that is the lumbar spine, started to cry out, she found it interesting that the part of the spine that holds the back and pelvis together, the very place that holds new life, was causing her severe pain. It had been a long time since she indulged in sexual activity as her husband had passed on and she had been preoccupied only with plans on how her children would join her in the United States. She was not surprised by the spine's rebellion for she had basically shut it down, only exercising it during her daily walks and while doing her house chores. She had taken it for granted, and now, she had been diagnosed with "spinal stenosis", an advanced degeneration of narrowing of the disc space. The disease was very painful and she could neither stand nor sit without feeling pains all over her body.

This became a "solid wall of fog" for Rita. She thought her effectiveness in the journey was diminishing due to energy drain from the pain. The cause, according to the doctor, was "mother nature", which could be how the spine was shaped from birth, less "bed exercise" and a "lot of work and age". All these hastened the effect of the stenosis.

Rita's whole body began to experience great pain and surgery, according to the doctor, would be a 50/50 chance. She was also told that the ailment may worsen after the surgery, which may confine her to a wheelchair for life. That notwithstanding, she was bent on continuing the journey including the inevitable goal of completing her doctorate degree programme which she had started on health care management. The journey had begun and she was neither going to look back nor allow anything to keep her off the shore; not even the fog. She will continue to climb the hill, focused, dependable and productive until she succeeds in achieving her dreams.

At a stage, the MRI result showed that her lower spine lumbar one to five were in a bad shape and needed immediate surgery. With this result, Rita requested to be transferred to another doctor. She got the transfer and a second doctor's opinion confirmed immediate surgery. The second doctor gave her the hope for a successful surgery and assured her that everything was going to be fine. The doctor immediately arranged for surgery and it was very successful as the doctor had promised. She was kept in the hospital and rehabilitation centre for many months.

In all these, Rita learnt that life can place a demand on anyone, but what matters most is how one acquiesce to the issue, succumbs to avoidance of opportunity or charts the course to stabilise and organise the process to the next level, trusting in and surrendering to the Almighty God.

After she was discharged from the hospital, Rita learnt that there are two important things in life; listening to one's heart and following one's own muse. Motherhood should not duck the tough issues; rather, it should face everything wisely and with a clear conscience.

Rita could not sit for long hours to write and continue her doctorate research, but resorted to lying on her stomach, with pillows to support her spine. This challenge never deterred her from getting to her destination. Instead, it made her to come to the understanding that life is limitless in expression and that the events of life will continue to unfold with divine potential. She continued with the battle and strived to make the world a better place for the new generation with confidence, knowing that there is a power more powerful than oneself, which one gets by trusting in the Almighty God.

Chapter Four

Rita decided to be on her own and exploit the facets of womanhood. She refused to join any African or Nigerian organisation in America. She had learnt from others that the terrain for these associations was sometimes complicated and cumbersome. Instead, she decided to continue to push on in the present, but it was one thing to be in the present and another to be welcomed into it without feeling lonely. In all the places she worked in the US, she felt out of place with the people young enough to be her children. She believed that nothing that happened should surprise her for she had learnt to accept with grace the gift her stay in the States offered. She must walk into this sacred spiral that had become a metaphor for the path she was now on and if she intended on changing her life, walking the labyrinth should offer her the very impetus she needed.

Those who had moved from Africa and other parts of the world to this great country, no matter their status or education, but without an American experience, she learnt, are meant to be leaving out something of them in the centre. Rita could not get the kind of job she anticipated and being with those who did not value the degree she had acquired, she had to enter into the same silent sanctuary and this made her feel like the child she once was. Playing bride to a fairy prince in the backyard, Rita was oblivious to anyone or anything save those who had known her once as a university professor in Africa. All of these forced her to further surrender to the process.

Although she got her degrees in the early eighties from a university in the US, she had no work experience with these degrees in America because she had left immediately after her graduation. Now, after eighteen-year of working in Nigeria, she could not fit into the system for lack of work experience. To get a good job in America would mean working continuously with your degrees for several years without a break. What is more, with an eighteen-year break in Nigeria, Rita was advised to enroll into any university to "bring back to life all her degrees" which she had obtained from the United States.

Back home in Nigeria and Africa in general, anyone with such degrees would not waste time getting a good job. But in America, without work experience for at least five years, it is hard to fit into any specialty, the type Rita was looking for.

Rita needed a job urgently to help her family back home in Nigeria, so she decided to take up any job that was offered to her. In effect, she decided to take off all manner of distraction so as not to lose her footing on such a narrow path. This logic, she thought, may stifle her journey, and she once again became totally present, but then she remembered what one of her mentors had said: 'Sometimes, the best thing that could happen to anyone in a cage would be for the "cage door to slam shut".' According to him, when this happens, 'one must move all the energies to the present and if one cannot go back, then one is forced to move forward. Rita felt energised as this gave her the hope to move on. The words of wisdom gave Rita the conviction that successful people go beyond the emotions of their failures. Her dedication to searching for any type of job would render the journey deliberate and patient. Also remembering that there is no maze set with dead ends, as all roads lead to the centre and cheating would only defeat the purpose, Rita decided to forget about all her degrees and, as such, she succeeded in getting a job at Wal-Mart. She then realised that "America is a leveler". While at work, sometimes, she looked around as she did her job, with self-consciousness, to see who might be watching her.

Rita would laugh at remembering that she was afterall on a mission, where no one was watching save herself and the Almighty God. She further relaxed into the experience, being grateful for all the steps she had taken on this journey. She continued working very hard, not minding the consequences and with time she moved up to a managerial position in the company. She also succeeded in getting a teaching job in the public school, but she remained at Wal-Mart as one of the part-time night managers. Rita later picked up another part-time job as a departmental manager in Lowes store, combining all these with the teaching job. At another time, she became a front end manager at Bloom. With all these, coupled with an inner peace for which she had no words to explain, she counted herself blessed.

With time, Rita got a second master's degree in Healthcare Management, and proceeded with her doctorate degree immediately in the same discipline. She encouraged herself to "stand sure", and gaze at the circle in which she was enclosed, knowing that there is no beginning or end to any circle. A circle is symbolic to life and as such consists of an endless continuum. Thus, Rita was able to discover so many aspects of herself in the journey, and this made her very happy.

Chapter Five

One of Rita's friends had convinced her to come out of her solitude and join the women association, which she had been hesitant to joining. Rita had wanted to stay in solitude to explore life and womanhood on her own. The physical incarceration of being single in the US without her children and other family relations, and the claustrophobic feeling of being alone for the rest of her life since her husband passed on, brought with it a heart-pounding and adrenaline-releasing fear of stepping into an unknown world. The loneliness Rita experienced made her feel silly. This forced her to agree to join the women association.

Her first time at the meeting took her down memory lane to Nigeria, where women sometimes congregate not knowing what to discuss. Instead of them to celebrate womanhood in a free foreign country, these women betrayed their values and picked on womanhood. They continued to blame the menfolk for their own inadequacies and an inability to unite as a strong union, thus disgracing womanhood. Rita saw the association as a disgrace.

Rita had learnt cultural transformation these past years. She has come to realise that people need a change of values to promote the kind of society they want; and the idea of communal values and the sense of mutual responsibility and social solidarity should be expressed not just in the church, mosque, neighbourhood, place of work, or within the family, but also through these associations. She believed in the power of culture to determine both individual success and social cohesion, especially when it concerns womanhood.

Rita noticed that people ignored these cultural factors at their peril but, instead, they pointed fingers and blamed others. It is important that womanhood should have a role in shaping culture for the better, but she wondered what made it so difficult for people to talk of values in ways that did not appear calculated. Maybe because these people had seen a lot in the culture where they came from or had become much scripted in their present circumstances. Rita was totally disappointed with the actions displayed at the meeting by the women and so she decided to withhold herself from such a group so that it would not corrupt the values she had so far acquired in her journey.

At the meeting, she had observed that members had no common ground in their discussions and no sense of mutual understanding. Their talk was cheap, like little children, and they seemed unaware of the fact that empathy must be acted upon. The women had forgotten that the next generation should be saddled with a good wealth of memories and legacies. To do otherwise would be to relinquish the best self of womanhood. Throughout the meeting, the women continued discussing irrelevances.

The journey so far had taught Rita that womanhood is full of optimism with green lights everywhere she goes and only pessimists see the red light. Rita truly agreed that men are the heads of every family but a woman who knows her worth can easily work underneath and make the strongest of men surrender to womanhood. It is not what one has to fight for, rather it is naturally endowed to womanhood. If not, why was Eve able to convince Adam when the instruction concerning the forbidden fruit was only given to the man alone? As a woman, one has to learn the way to manoeuvre humanity for good and indirectly rule the community.

During the meeting, Rita became totally lost, enough to find herself missing out in all the women's discussions. The members continued dancing around without any solid point and treading on the back road of consciousness, circumventing issues. As such, Rita took the dismal thoughts as she sat Indian style on her chair with eyes closed, rocking back and forth. She had shut her mind off from the happenings around her, which was often the game of deception she played with herself.

When there was no nerve to cover the women's behaviour, Rita opened her eyes, brought out the crucifix in her handbag and looked at it, dumbfounded. She sat in that state, at a crossroads. She hesitated a moment inwardly for womanhood inspiration to give her guidance. Staring at the cross in her hand and thinking that she must be at a crossroad, one of which represented the past she would never return to two other possibilities remained, but their outcome was unknown. A quiet presence overtook her and her pulse slowed. She tried to get her hands relaxed but her palms opened spasmodically. As she gained a blessed clarity, she grabbed her car key and walked out of the meeting hall.

'Are you kidding me?' Rita whispered to herself. 'What exactly is wrong with African womanhood?' she questioned the empty air in front of her. She really was not concerned about the popular culture any more, for motherhood had so far taught her how to create her own realm; a realm of actions and words without owning any terrain. How can the women continue to blame the men in the women association in the United States of America?

'Women should go out and own what they deserve with silent actions,' she spoke out loud.

At that instant, contacts with the world she had left behind got her confused and getting up, all she remembered was walking to the car while trying for her life's sake to control the anger lurching in her stomach. She was frightened and full of anger. Revisiting the past was not something she did frequently, but only in her dreams where she had no control over the memories that drifted into her mind. She never wanted to go back to the bad experience she had in Nigeria for this would traumatise her.

In the car, Rita tried to calm herself but hesitated for a moment before heading away from the meeting venue. As she left the meeting, she began to think more clearly. She slot into her car stereo the CD of Anna Mwalagho's song, "The Women of the World." The song was about the women that had made it in the world. She took a deep breath and wished for calmness to overwhelm her while she drove home. There and then she decided never to attend the women's meeting again.

The next morning, Rita woke up slowly, trying to remember what had happened the previous day. She started to feel her fate in what she could not fear and learnt to move where she had to go. In such a short space of time, she had learnt that in America, the relationship between manhood and womanhood is like reaching a destination of intersection where an east-to-west road crosses a north-to-south one, the two routes running in different directions to meet at a mutual point of contact and neither road changing direction. This mutual point is for all men and women which enables all to reach their destinations. Within this crossroads and intersection, is the point of unity where humanity naturally meets. This is the height of connections, influence, creativity and convergence that elevates and escalates womanhood to ascend an airspace specially created as an advantage for the female species.

The special height is given to womanhood for bringing new lives and new generations. It helps womanhood to inspire and nurture babies that would become adults. It is a weapon specially given to womanhood to pass to all humanity for use in exploring and exploiting the mother earth. This is truly a spice strongly routed in all women, for motherhood's DNA, gene and blood are strongly stamped into all mankind. Every human being is stamped with the blood of a mother for nine months or more in the womb. This is a prize God has given to all humanity for further inventions from the woman's blood for generations to come. So womanhood should never be intimidated.

Chapter Six

When Rita lost her younger brother, a delegate of the women association came to pay their condolences. Immediately she saw them, her heart began to beat fast and her blood pressure rose. She was never a member of their association, but they needed to take her back with this visit. The delegate consisted of the president of the association, other executives and members of the association. They brought her lots of things and made her understand that the women had taken a decision to move ahead peacefully as a group without involving the men. They convinced her to come back to the association.

At the first visit to the association after the delegation's visit, Rita noticed that the women all worked with one accord. She was very happy with them and advised them to continue moving on. She agreed to begin to attend the meetings regularly once more. Since she was not living in the state where the association was situated, she presumed all the women were moving on as they had told her. The first few meetings she attended were interesting and very peaceful, but she was still skeptical, remembering what Machiavelli said in *The Princely Virtues*: 'There never was a man more effective in swearing that things were true and greater the oaths with which he made a promise, the less he observed it.' According to the book, human nature will 'always succeed, because he thoroughly understands many aspects of human mind.'

The saying reminded Rita of the human mind and her experience with the women of her home town in Nigeria; the women she had worked with, loved but could never emulate. They were dignified women she respected but whose fates did not align with her own. It was into that creation of womanhood that she took all attributes she sought for in herself, but she concluded that the past was a memory and every new day should be a rebirth. She tried not to remember how the women disappointed her and how they deserted all their accomplishments to disgrace womanhood. She felt like laughing aloud. 'Will history repeat itself?' she questioned herself. She doubted it.

The journey into womanhood had accorded her the opportunity to think about love, forgiveness, loyalty and ways to keep her own heritage and virtue. Rita remembered what a physician, Richard Swenson, had said: 'A broken relationship is like a razor across the artery of the spirit, even when it is amended, sometimes the bleeding never stops.' It is reconciliation that will bring wholeness, and according to Condoleezza Rice: 'One has to be open to serendipity and continue moving forward.' Although we cannot guarantee people's dependability, it is important to discern between sincerity and truthfulness and the best way to do this is to set appropriate boundaries, which will involve adequate rules and regulations. Rita had to reconstitute ways to give these women everything without losing her own identity in the process.

She remembered what she had told them at their last meeting that it was not important to argue about authority in the family. Let the man know he is always in charge. Accord him his respect as the Commander-in-Chief, but underneath, the woman should use her wit to rule the home. Arguing about authority and leadership often brings about divorce and separation. But a positive woman's behaviour and actions could control the man and the entire community. Womanhood should make the man succumb to the woman's authority with her good actions. A man's strength and masculinity will only be mellowed by keeping womanhood in charge of affairs in the home.

Nature had designed men to be more powerful physically and the most powerful man can be brought down to his knees by an articulate witty woman. Euripides, the wife of Jason in the story of Medea, reminded everyone that womanhood skills are dangerous as each human being is born of a woman. She said: 'Women, though most helpless in doing good deeds, are the cleverest of contrivers (Euripides' *Medea*, 480-406 BC).'

Many of the women approached Rita to contest for the post of the president. She bluntly refused because she wanted to remain an observer in the association. After several meetings with the women, and a lot of wise suggestions, many began contacting her to take up the offer of running for the presidency, but she could not come to terms with herself to accept the offer because she had a preconceived idea of how it might turn out. Many of the women were disappointed. The president herself called on Rita urging her to accept to contest for the post. She assured Rita that her wisdom and tenacity were what could help the women's association to continue to move forward. But Rita turned down her request, and continued to study them, analysing the women individually and as a group.

She realised that most of the women, by their behaviours were like children, who had mastered the tools of survival in their tightly-bound world in the United States and made no apologies for it. They had come to the United States very young and did not have any knowledge on how to handle African men and women associations. Many arrived in America to join their husbands at tender ages, went to school, had babies and got good jobs. This group of women were not used to the hard life in Africa with the culturally-bound men and women learning to master how to manoeuvre their lives in the culture and live peacefully and wisely with other members of the family.

With Rita's wealth of experience and vast activities with African women's associations back home in Nigeria, and now in the US, she concluded that these ladies and herself were two worlds apart. Many of them were divorced or separated from their husbands because of these two worlds they had encountered in the US. The key was not to try to match the men's venom, instead, it was having the wisdom to crawl inside the man with a motherhood psyche and take control of the family, thereby making the man worship womanhood indirectly.

Each culture is unique and so motherhood has to master the rubrics and ways to win in the African family setting. The problem that erupts is giving the men their respect and at the same time standing firm on womanhood virtues. This could have gained the women everything they needed. It is unique with African culture and in fact with all cultures, as womanhood silently directs and rules the world. Womanhood had to be right back there in that pituitary without so much as a noise.

After the meeting, Rita went home and her spirit directed her to accept the offer to run for the post of the president of the association. That night, she could not sleep. A line of questions on what seemed like a silent visionless sea went through her mind. She knew something must be wrong because the sea cannot be visionless, hence she looked for signs. What do these signs look like? She thought about the girls in the university, the women in her home town who were being intimidated because of their sex, and the children that do not have access to education back home. She thought of what formal education would do for these children and women. It would help them to understand the real world they should be living; their actual culture and community as God had created it, not the world where women and children do not have any say or contribution to make. But a world of equality, freedom of speech and liberty. A world where love is expressed in several ways and not through intimidation;

the promise of being part of something and of mastering the environment. This is what will make everyone happy and long to live in harmony. She could be the one to begin this in her community, Rita thought.

Young girls need to have women who would stand in as their mentors and show them examples of motherhood outside their mothers. Women who do not have any stake on how they turn out, who can encourage them to take risks and who would pick them up when they fall flat on their face would be what they need. Young boys that are confused, rejected and denied of a good life need role models who would help them develop positive self-esteem while growing up. Children need to have people to look up to in a society where disparity between men and women is rampant. Rita's hope is to give hope to these "hopeless women and children" where they are neglected, treated with disdain, violated and abandoned.

Many young men are left with violent tendencies as a way of life in many places in Africa especially in Nigeria. This has become rampant in third world countries, thereby destroying the African society because there is no one to guide male children through the process of becoming men, and no one to explain to them the meaning of manhood.

In the university, Rita had tried to expose her students, both male and female, to a lot of things in life and had also given them different value orientations, something to counteract the materialism, individualism and instant gratification rampant in society. In the African culture, respect for elders is important, be it male or female, in giving young people a base for themselves and not as a basis to denigrate manhood or womanhood. Unless the young ones are rooted in this type of tradition, they would not be able to appreciate what other cultures have to offer. Many of Rita's colleagues in the university, where she taught "Nigerian Peoples and Culture", and some men in her community felt threatened by Rita's teaching, and thought she was going against the values of her culture. Nevertheless, this did not stop her from doing what she had to do with her students to inculcate in them the idea of gender equality. Rita believed that a garden will always have weeds and pests, and may even have pestilence to contend with once in a while. But with the right combination of elements, pollination by bees and butterflies and a good gardener, it will become a place of sensuality and balance.

Thinking of all these, Rita was able to calm herself and go back to sleep that night. She woke up the next morning and called the president to inform her of her willingness to contest for the next election as the president of the organisation. The president was very happy and began campaigning for Rita. During the election, she won with a wide margin as almost all the women voted for her.

As she sat with the women after the election, her thoughts returned to that period in her home town when the women decided to abandon the women's meeting to join the men's. She could vividly see the faces of those women she had left behind back home now. But Rita encouraged herself to continue moving forward because no one can ever go back to fix the past. With that in mind, she focused on the present and asked herself, 'What would she expect from these women that had such trust in her? What does she hope to gain for womanhood with the association?'

Experience had taught Rita that if she decides to wait for the perfect moment when all is safe and assured, it may never come; neither would mountains be climbed, races run nor lasting happiness achieved for no human can act beyond his or her level of consciousness. She must immediately have the right focus on womanhood as maturity and ideas change with time. She had to let these women know that the precious resources that motherhood have are not only around them but inside of them.

After the election that evening, Rita found out that so many organisations had broken off from the mother wing to form other women's social clubs. At this point, Rita told herself that she had the responsibility to redeem her time. She decided to set the goals immediately to show the world who she was, and how far she had come. 'It is good to accept challenges and never be put down in whatever one has accepted to do,' she assured herself.

Rita's mind went back to the cross which she had and she became enticed by its design, many of which looked like two unbroken circles placed side by side, a symbol of infinity. As she glanced at the cross, it reminded her that reciprocity is important because no one can survive alone. She imagined what side of the cross she would be taking with these women for there was something in every corner of the cross. But she still believed that the glory of her experience would be found in the element of the surprises she would meet.

Rita realised her childhood instincts were right because her whole goal had been to penetrate patriarchy as a woman. To achieve this, she believed that what she had to do was to inspire young people, who are the future generation. Her desire, pledge and wish must be to remember the true nature of womanhood. The divine light which womanhood carries within herself is inherited from God himself and part of the light which makes women so magnificent is the blessing and gift of womanhood.

With the above in mind, she reflected on what Senator Hillary Clinton said to Senator Barack Obama during the 2008 democratic election: 'When the phone rings at three o'clock in the morning, who would be most adept to answer the call?' This could symbolise womanhood being on guard from the first day she brings a new life into the world. With the crying of the child during the night through to the early hours of the morning, the mother is up and alert, ready to nurture and protect humanity so as to preserve the next generation. The "call" may be a cause through problems, needs or conflicts and the woman who shies away from such turbulence is not meant to be called a "mother" because she would despair and speculate instead of doing what needs to be done. The "call" may be a very crucial period to speculate a line of action that would save the family or world from crisis. How motherhood responds to trials of family life and copes with nurturing the species she brings to the world reveals what stuff she is made of. Motherhood is divinely imbued with the new generation by the Creator himself.

Chapter Seven

Rita thanked the women for their support and trust and reminded them that they were all on a special journey in the United States of America. She expressed how humbled and highly honoured she was to have gotten to that phase of the journey as a woman from their community back in Nigeria. She reminded them that it was an exciting moment in history for womanhood with heightened awareness to embrace change in freedom of thought, passion and purpose; a prewired gift from God Himself to women and all mankind. Motherhood is designed thoughtfully and wonderfully to journey, soaring limitlessly in all areas of this life and taking with it new generations which will create credible changes in every culture. This is the journey which has taken womanhood from Africa to the new world, coupled with truthfulness, new ideas and new concepts. Therefore, it was important that every woman remained vigilant to the changes happening around the world.

Rita further assured the women that she had accepted to serve them because she was sure all would work together as a group of wonderful ladies who were blessed by the Almighty God and dedicated to the future generation of their country, Nigeria, and Africa as a whole. She warned that the journey might not be easy and smooth. There might be a few who would not agree with every decision and policy she would be making, but if all would work with one spirit and stand on a common ground of agreement, the next generation of children would benefit. If all the women were united as sisters from the same state in Nigeria and work with one mind, there would be greater achievement. Rita told them that she believes winners have two things in common; definite goals and a burning desire to achieve these goals. She proceeded to list the goals they were to achieve, which were:

- To further the existing legacies of their predecessors.
- To source funds, aids and other resources from local and international agencies so as to better the lives of young children through interactions with local and international organisations such as the World Bank, schools, universities and hospitals.
- To work on creating awareness through gender equality programmes.
- To continue in the charity projects the women had started.

With all these, Rita urged each member to think of projects that would help their great country, Nigeria and the communities where they resided in the US. She further stressed that to achieve these goals they must be able to make some sacrifices by sowing seeds of hard work, having love for one another and having a forgiving heart.

She reminded the women that in many associations, especially back in Nigeria, gender mainstreaming is often evident in all policies and programmes. This is why in Nigerian villages, towns and even churches, there are men's groups and women's groups. Each of these groups is independent of the other, but they work in cooperation with one another to achieve a common goal for society. The Igbo culture already recognised the need for women to work independently but in cooperation with the menfolk. Women would respect and recognise the men. If these men would at any time need the women's help and cooperation, they would not hesitate to be at their service. Rita emphasised that the men will also recognise the women as independent and both would work together with respect for each other. Their greatest strength would be the love all would have for their roots – Nigeria and Africa. With this in mind, each person must work to build unity and respect for the group.

She further stressed that good relationship was important for the fulfilment and enhancement of the expanding community of all people in Nigeria and those in the diaspora. She highlighted that it was important to build a strong network that would cut across all people, in spite of facing different directions or having diverse perspectives. She told the women that when people are united, they stand, but if they are divided, they fall. The women in the whole of the United States of America are one and should not be divided. Doors of opportunities will be open to all women who share this dream of a better Nigeria, because this dream comes from the heart of selfless service for all womanhood.

Rita further urged the women to move with their heads held higher and their shoulders squarer as they celebrate womanhood. She assured them that they would all put their heads together to tackle unemployment, improve education and promote good health in Nigeria as well as encourage peaceful coexistence among Nigerians and those in the diaspora. Rita ended her speech by assuring the women that every effort would aim to bring hope to all children and to write their names in the annals of Nigerian history, thus promoting womanhood.

After addressing the women, everything that happened reminded Rita that life is like a stage; like the spring flower, and one emerges from it as the flower blooms. When the season is bountiful, it is important to continue heading forward, playing one's part without wasting time, whether old or young, because the season may be very short-lived. As the days go by, it would be difficult to look back or cry over past events. Instead, it is better to move on with definite plans which should be executed immediately, otherwise the days may go by and then comes the next season. In the new season, someone else steps in to play his or her part and if this is done well, the former is forgotten and a new life begins and so it continues. Thus, one is only remembered by the good works one does for humanity.

In this life's journey, womanhood should be ready and strong. Even when a woman relaxes in sleep, her subconscious mind should continue working. If any new idea comes to mind, at whatever hour of the night, it is important to wake up and put it in writing so that the idea does not slip away. This may be very helpful for the journey of womanhood and could serve as a stepping stone for the new generation.

Chapter Eight

At the end of that meeting, one of the women rushed to the new president as she was about to get into her car and whispered, 'Are you aware that the past president removed money from the corporate account belonging to the Women's Wing and opened a new account?'

Rita did not understand what the lady meant but it came like a powerful message available only in a place where strife is more common than peace, where impermanence reigns and lives.

This lady looked straight into Rita's eyes and emphasised, 'I have to warn you as the new president to be ready because the Women's Wing is still in full swing. And those women are ready to sue this association in court so as to get their money back,' she added and quietly disappeared.

Rita had learnt from the journey that when someone advises, first try to balance the perspective effectively and then carry out an appraisal of what has been said, including the source before assimilating what it is. It struck Rita that her own association must be a faction of the Women's Wing if the main association was still on as this woman had said. She sat quietly for what seemed like eternity, probably not more than twenty seconds, in her car. Then she asked herself some questions to know if her brain was falling asleep. She moved her toes but felt no pain. Her mind had wondered off a bit but she became aware of her surroundings again. Hastily, Rita stored that information in the inaccessible part of her brain where one puts the memory of pain and other unpleasantness.

She started the car, deciding not to think about what she had heard. As she drove home, she played her best music, trying to find peace. Rita decided to neither call any member nor discuss what she had heard with anyone, and presumed that if it was true, other women must surely know about it and so would bring it up in the next meeting.

As the organisation progressed, a lot of things started to unfold, which she never knew were there. At one of the meetings, she listened as the past president narrated how she had taken the decision to open a new account with the money from the Women's Wing's account. She also spoke about renaming the association's account instead of "Women's Wing" that it was. She had registered the new association under a new name, signed a new article of incorporation and further told all the members that the old association was moving on as before without the men. She never confided nor discussed this with any member of the new association. She said she did this to protect the women because 'of the problems the women's wing was having with the men's wing,' and that the association had to move on, though with the same abbreviation as before.

Some of the women who did not agree with her had stayed back in the old association with her vice president and the men. They continued as Women's Wing. This action and behaviour of the past president got many of the women confused. Rita immediately remembered her position as the organiser of Anambra Women back in Nigeria when she was working with the government of the state. 'Could such thing ever happen?' she questioned. 'Never!' She boldly told the women that it was a wrong decision and what the past president did could not be ruled out.

As the new president, Rita knew the association was in grave danger and for it to survive, she had to find the best solution and move fast to correct the mishap done. The organisation must have to cut through the intensity of this crisis and respond with strength and urgency. If the association must move on as the past president had said, members must agree and act immediately. The thought of losing what the association already had left Rita with the tenacity to start thinking of what must be done so as to move forward. She had come to realise that there were great battles, conflicts and challenges to surmount and she would need strength for the journey. She concluded that she had to trust God for strength and wisdom, else she would become confused and fumble.

Unfortunately, because many women had decided to stay back in the old association, the Women's Wing, this made things worse. Rita had presumed there was no other women's group other than the present association, which the past president had maintained, and all the women were working together. This made Rita feel befuddled and so she could not decide whether to obey her heart or her head. It would be too late to back out from the association because she had been sworn in as the new president. It became clear to Rita that the reality of her amazing days had been dissolved in the US and the comfort of her seclusion in the journey disturbed. She quietly started looking inwardly for more inspiration on how to tackle the problem. Confronted with these tensions, Rita decided to fast and pray more, knowing that her strength would only come from the Almighty God. Thus, she remembered what a James Taylor said: 'Try to be rescued and surround yourself with good people. Take time to solitude.' At that, she attached herself to God Almighty.

Rita, in her solitude, thought of the principle she initially espoused and at that her mind toured from the world of action to the realm of reasoning and back again. This reflection would only require an interlocutor, someone who reasoned on the same frequency with her. Sometimes the interlocutor could better be imagined than real, as when one argued with oneself, knowing that spirituality would be the answer.

A big problem had been passed on to Rita and this problem must be solved. Rita decided to be calm and in a flash and with a lot of clarity, a lot of ideas came to her mind. She decided to put her feelings aside until she mastered everything, knowing that acceptance does not mean that one agrees with, condones, appreciates, or even likes what has happened.

Rita was able to put what she was experiencing into some kind of context to gain perspective of the whole situation. She began to feel a wave of melancholy sweeping over her as she shrank back into silence in most of the meetings and such periods could never be compared with the extraordinary journey which she had taken.

Rita, from experience, had mastered the reward one gets from listening as well as speaking. All the women had refused to accept her suggestions and many of them opposed every suggestion and decisions she presented as the new president while a majority of the women sided with the past president.

This reminded Rita of what Socrates said in Plato's Republic where he compared ordinary citizens to a group of prisoners confined in a cave. The people in the cave had only seen all through their life's time the play of shadows on the wall and a reflection of objects they never apprehended. Only 'the philosopher/leader on this account could ascend from the cave to the bright sunlight of the day where she would see things as they really are.' This would happen if the philosopher/leader is able to coax back into the darkness where the cave dwellers lived to convince the people of the true light. Rita as the new president could be that philosopher/leader, but how can she convince them of the reality? This became a big question for her.

Rita had been schooled from birth to hide her emotions, so she began to regard the women steadily because she was becoming suffocated by their behaviours.

After several meetings and learning many more lies that led to the disintegration of the main association, the Women Wing, Rita recoiled to study the main character, the past president and her motherhood leadership style. This happened when Rita was able to think clearly and had reached a level where she was content with her energy, for there are many battles not worth fighting openly.

Rita noticed that the past president was ambitious, intelligent and very articulate, but she lacked the ability to understand the different soul and gender elements. She was smart, smug and completely happy with herself. The past president knew how to make her inner voice meet, fight love and co-create. She was that type of woman in one's neighborhood who often stops by a neighbour's garden and gets the neighbour going on an idea she wants from her about her flower garden. Later, when the neighbour walks by the woman's garden, she gets to discover the most spectacular flower, not exactly what she planted, but something that shows the influence of the tips the two had discussed earlier.

The past president was someone that was very open to the world so that she could better create a microcosm of her own; someone that had confronted the common problems of all those who fought for gender equality. Though she had faced a society that deifies and undervalues that role, she had worked with collaborators to balance her personal and public life. There was more to this lady than met the eyes.

Rita wanted to find out how this lady's experience connected to motherhood in doing symbolic work and how her actions related to the larger matters of creativity, especially with women. This became a difficult task for Rita to comprehend. As someone who studied psychology and philosophy, Rita was interested in the composition of people beyond what was obvious. That was why while studing people, she pretended to be a novice, a co-creator in her own way. This was one reason she was drawn to personality architecture, to study what people are made of and why they behave the way they do; how they invite people in and why people are drawn to them. The study allowed Rita to become interested the moment she encountered a new life. She was known to never allow people's nature incarcerate her thinking by forcing their opinions on her. Rita would rather remain quiet and listen in case she could gain some wisdom that could influence her but would never allow other people's opinions or ideas to control her.

The character of the past president was the type that played with an archetype. Rita noticed that sometimes this lady controlled others out of fear and felt she had to be on the "highway" at all times and if she was not, the whole system would collapse. When a character embodies this archetype, some people see it as emanating a supernatural presence. This is an obvious example of the past president; she was not mistaken. It was almost as if she carried that lineage of leadership of women's affair with her. She stepped into it and realised others around her needed to keep her there.

The past president had been labelled strong and resilient; two admirable qualities that had been her undoing. Ultimately, she could not separate herself from the world and herself because she was a controller and so she did all the work by herself. Oddly, these qualities had blinded her when Rita came into the scene and had been very careful not to buy into that moment of projection; the idea that forms when such a leader is having a relationship with the people. Rita was aware that when a leader starts believing what she is not, she offends the divine nature in others. It is best for womanhood leadership to learn to surrender to the moment, because 'destiny will always win'. This reminded Rita of what happened in the play, *Julius Caesar* when Mark Anthony commented in his speech that 'The evil that men do lives after them; the good is oft interred with their bones. So let it be with Caesar...'

Rita had learnt that leadership needs to cut through the intensity of crisis and respond with strength, agility and urgency, minimising damages and maximising opportunities. As a leader, true motherhood has to eat some humble pie and know that it is only part of a creative process. Motherhood leadership should remember that she is only privileged to be a part, and not entirely the source. One can only tap into the source, but if one's leadership gets wrapped up in its own personality, one might not feel it. When the leader is not truly connected to what is given her but concentrates with force, using the image of power, frequency and ease with which some people have projected her to 'try on a pair of her own sandals or shoes in leadership', she will surely fail. Rita realised that this was the reason why the women's wing of the association fell apart during the past president's tenure and the men took advantage of the situation.

Though the past president happened to be a very lovely lady, she often tried to control humanity without learning the rubrics, especially on how to control people with more sophisticated psychological and physiological background, which had resulted in the failure of the organisation. The past president with her own psyche controlled the women quite well and Rita observed that she did not want to step aside completely. No matter who was the new president, she still wanted to control the leadership and the whole organisation in her own way. As such, everything must be in accordance with her decisions. But she missed out on Rita's quiet demeanour for she did not understand Rita's type.

The past president did not understand that leaders must learn to study how to manage the 'dismal, the distracted and the dangerous' in every organisation. It is very important for womanhood leadership to view impositions and oppositions as opportunities to test their strength, exercise their talents and expand their visions. This is what helps in nurturing the new generation. With this in mind, Rita being the new president, had decided to keep a good frame of mind while she waited, rather than to manipulate. She knew that motherhood should be honest to find the quality that scored within her when she was able to crawl inside the new association. So Rita stopped judging and decided to find that place where she could do the things that could horrify the whole association.

Motherhood leadership has to find out the victim in people, get the ego out of them and tame it. If motherhood does not do that, the natural DNA in the next generation will unfortunately erupt and the whole community will be in disarray. Motherhood as a leader should stand strong when the wind blows, whether gently or with a bitter blast. She has to take her time to understand the bearing, hiding her seal to give the new generation hope for she is greater than life itself.

The past president had refused to hand over the organisation to the new executives and her hesitation did not bother Rita. But after a big fight, the handing over was reluctantly done. It was then the new president noticed that the new association was created the same month the money belonging to the corporate unit of the old association was removed from the bank without the consent of the members. The election for the new executives took place the following month. After a few months that same year, the past president received a letter from the attorney of the old association asking her to return the money she took or be taken to court.

The article of incorporation of the new association had been renewed bearing the past president's name as still the president and the new executives were elected and sworn in. Rita, being the new president, tried to avoid being quick to take sides in battles that started before she joined up in the association.

A lot of stories were coming up, so Rita decided to contact and communicate with the leader of the women's wing privately in order to learn the truth rather than making enemies. Though Rita knew that keeping boundaries was necessary at that point, this might limit her ability to know the truth. With the set adventure, Rita became confused because getting into a new territory would need thorough survey as she did not know the lady before then other than the stories she had heard from other women. Rita needed to know who this lady was and the attitude she possessed. As such, she started by first studying the topographic and geographical indicators that would lead her to the lady.

Rita then went ahead to contact other people who knew the women's wing leader very well, knowing that human nets are very important. She remembered what one of her mentors had said: 'Human nets can capture, contain and convey more than any single string.' Rita did a thorough background check and got shocking diverse stories about her new association, from this lady. With all the facts that she had gathered, and without the knowledge of other members, Rita held strong to her base, remaining calm and confident because she realised that in order to get along with the association, she could not afford to lose herself.

After the investigations, Rita kept everything to herself and advised members of the association to swallow their pride and go back to the parent body, the Women's Wing.

She also advised that they return everything they took from them, then they could fight to share the money. This created numerous frictions, arguments, disunity and anarchy among the members. Many members began to distance themselves from active participation because of the court case.

As this was going on, an important personality from the men's group wrote what got Rita's attention. He said when people form an association that is not directed towards an illegal purpose and does not seek illegal ways to attain its objectives, such an association cannot be put to trial. He went further to say that their association started as a family friendship group, and later became a successful organisation. He lamented that it was the jostling for leadership positions by both men and women that was killing the association. He then appealed to all members to try and fix the world within themselves, then the world without would be fine.

With such a brilliant and intelligent advice from this man, Rita totally agreed with him. On the same ground, Oswald Chambers had once said that people are always looking for justice, yet the essence of the teaching of the "Sermon on the Mount" is 'Never look for justice, but never cease to give it.'

Rita's anxiety increased as each day passed and she began to repeat what Martin Luther King Jr. said every day: 'Power at its best is love implementing the demands of justice, and justice at its best is power correcting everything that stands against love.'

As the new president of the association, Rita believed that the money belonged to their state back home in Nigeria, and it would be better to focus on the issues and ways that would move the people forward individually and collectively, than investing in a court case. She told the women that taking that money from the main association to start a new one was against the law. It was just like someone who has been employed to work for a company and after helping to raise funds to expand the company, resigns and leaves with all the furniture and funds she has accrued for the office and goes ahead to establish a new company with a different name but the same abbreviation as the old one. Not stopping there, she gets a new tax identification number for the new company, whearas the money used had been earmarked for a different tax identification number. 'This was a fraudulent behaviour,' Rita told the women.

The journey had taught Rita that everything in a woman's life will touch other territories especially the new generation. Motherhood had to balance her intellect with inspiration for the next generation which would be her offspring. Thinking through the possible options and solutions to the problems, Rita's mind was focused on motherhood and the new generation of Nigerians back home and in the diaspora.

Chapter Nine

Returning the money to where it belonged and pulling the women out from court became Rita's primary objective. Deep down in her spirit, she felt she was divinely made the president of the association at that particular time for a reason and that was to fight for motherhood, and failing to do so might attract God's wrath. During those times, she thought of what Ralph Waldo Emerson had said:

> It is easy in the world to live after the world's opinion; it is easy in solitude to live after our own; but the great man is he who in the midst of the crowd keeps with perfect sweetness the independence of solitude.

As Rita sat in solitude pondering on Emerson's statement, she let a benign smile lift the corners of her lips as she remembered the cross hanging before her. She felt people spend the most part of their lives unlearning the rules, conditions and goals that were set for them by other people. These people take time to become matured enough to rediscover themselves – the person that he or she was born to be. The fact that many individuals are striving toward unknown ends is what is so striking in this life's journey. Womanhood is born for change. No matter how long one had been screwed up, one must be friendly with oneself and try to conquer every obstacle and destiny. Lastly, one must not try to live another person's life.

The centre of the cross helped Rita to believe that acceptance of the truth with one's conscience is the biggest stretch each person has to extend to another. It is the strength womanhood has to acquire or risk being estranged from the tides of life's journey.

Rita had suggested to the women many ways and drawn up many plans the new association could use to raise funds but they had refused to listen and continued with the court case. She then began planning how to return the money to the corporate body, because a lifelong habit of vast reading and the wisdom gained from it had taught her to accept challenges. With that, she approached some members of the association privately and made some suggestions, but they were also not ready to support her ideas and this left her at a crossroads. Rita began to panic. The still small voice in her continued to urge her to act and not wait on her association's support, while the demonic voice attacking her from many angles urged her not to act. But Rita once again resorted to praying and trusting in God. The good voice challenged her to do the right thing, with the assurance of getting help to overcome the fear, anger and shame that might follow. At that point, she made up her mind on what to do.

Rita did not wait for anyone to tell her how or when to take action. She only discussed her next move with her inner spirit and took the decision to execute her plans. She went to the bank all by herself, withdrew the whole money belonging to the corporate association of the women, made the money order in the name, "Women's Wing", and took it straight to the court with a signed letter. Getting there, she deposited the money with the authorities of the court, to be left in an escrow account as the case was still in progress.

She took this initiative to return all that was removed from the corporate body by the past president including all the equipment, with a notarised letter to the justice of the court because it was the right thing to do. She hoped her actions would bring an end to the lawsuit that had divided their community in the diaspora and get her people united once again.

The lawsuit had negatively impacted the brotherly and sisterly relationship of every Nigerian in the United States of America. But Rita's action gave her a joyful exuberance and special confidence in defending womanhood. It also exhilarated her soul to soar because she had chosen to fight a noble battle when she knew she was right. When she looked back, 'There's not much I wouldn't have done all over again,' she told herself. This was because she had come to know that the practice of forgiveness is the ticket to clarity, vitality and freedom.

The critics and skeptics, together with their attorney, threatened and tried to frighten Rita with another lawsuit. They made a lot of noise but Rita was confident and neither paid any attention to all their threats nor allowed their criticism to deter her. This was because she knew that since her influence and intellect had now evolved, she could move forward without people criticizing her.

Rita was sure trying to get people to see who she was truly was not the right use of energy. She had no control, and they didn't see that; and why would she want them to? Where would it stop? These women had never walked and lived in the wisdom that she had, and would never have the same sight as she did. At that, Rita remembered that when motherhood collides with those whose sights are limited by the views they have of the world, it is a futile exercise to expect them to see what she sees. The Almighty God created women to partake of the wisdom and heights which would allow them to have children who will continue to impact future generations, exploring and discovering many unforeseeable things that are kept for mankind. Rita believed that the height of her womanhood ideas and creativity would always converge to elevate her to where other species would not be able to compete with her. That is why nature has made it that only womanhood can carry her baby for nine months and nurture it to exploit what is hidden in creation as the years go by. Her loving and adoring silence, with sensitive and immense goodness, should be used to temper the universe. That was the same situation between Rita and the women, for though they all belonged to the same association, they did not have the same sight, wisdom, perspective, maturity and experiences which Rita had received from God. She refused to stoop so low as to battle with them in the court.

This could have made Rita to lose her leverage and land her on her back, becoming a disgrace to womanhood.

Sometimes, it is good to defend motherhood in its entirety. She had learnt that there are moments when motherhood had to make peace when people are at war, and fight those who love to conquer all. Though the women had known Rita for a few years as their new president, within that short period she had opened up and undressed the obvious questions about womanhood to them.

The mother association immediately wrote the breakaway one that the case was being pulled out of court as the money and all property had been returned to them. But the past president of the new association and some of the women refused to back down. They rallied a few of the women to ban Rita from the association. The past president became the new president of the association as she had wished and continued with the court case.

Rita honourably resigned her presidency and pulled out from the association. The jury finally reached a verdict on the case and convicted all the women, founding them guilty. The money and every other thing relinquished were returned to them by the court immediately with a court order.

Rita did not count this as victory because they all came from Nigeria. Rather, she saw it a loss to womanhood. But there had been a few critical times when her actions met her approval and this was one of them. Rita boldly congratulated herself. If these women had listened to her advice, they would have appreciated the gift given to womanhood and learnt the rubrics and beauty given to them as mothers of the earth. This reminded Rita that 'the arc of moral universe is long but in one way or the other, it bends towards justice,' according to Martin Luther King Jr.

In every fight, Rita had learnt to stay on the right path no matter how difficult that path might be. This is because even at the lowest moment, it will never be compared to what one will lose when one fights not as a woman of integrity.

The outcome of the case showed that a woman of integrity would use an inner eye to visualise the future because God had stamped in every woman a special DNA that rules the universe and it depends on the woman to discover what she has and make positive use of it. This became a big lesson for all, especially Africans at home and in the diaspora. Because the moment a human being becomes arrogant and thinks that his or her plans are infallible, that is the moment such is likely to start falling. To succeed in any organisation, it is important to learn to keep the eyes on the right track and remain truthful at all times, trusting that God never made a mistake in creating womanhood.

As the president, Rita had no fear with the decision she had made because she never made the destination of her journey more important than the journey itself. Her plan instead was to begin a journey with the fear of God. The journey on this planet continues to unfold according to the amount of time one has and at the pace God had designed it to move. If it is the path of one's destiny and what God has planned, one will not be too late or too early, but will accomplish exactly what is intended.

Rita pictured the new association and thought her predecessor must have been amazed by the verdict of the court. Tension, she presumed, must have distorted their statues to cause confusion amongst the members, but for Rita, the road was less rocky. With time, the association disintegrated and many of the women returned to the mother association. With all that happened Rita had come to realise that in the journey of womanhood, life begins to end the day a mother becomes silent about those things that matter.

Chapter Ten

Rita was overwhelmed with joy that justice had prevailed and womanhood had been rescued. Well-meaning people both at home and in the diaspora appreciated Rita's honesty and had a great deal of admiration for her integrity. So many wanted to know who she was and wished for more of people of such character that resolutely refused to act disingenuously as human nature would demand. She decided to join the main association in America to continue the journey and was given a higher post. This exposed her to the national body of the association in the whole of America and she was happier working for her people at a higher level.

The news of Rita's actions and success got to her home town and to the governor of her state in Nigeria. She received several recognitions, plaques and appreciation from her people. All the town's people especially the women as well and the traditional leader were very proud of her. They congratulated and honoured her for standing for the truth. She was given a special chieftaincy title, which was a rare recognition for a woman in the Nigerian culture. This qualified her to sit with kingmakers and other highly-placed decision makers. Her name was also registered in the Nigerian Government Gazette, a vital document at home and in Africa.

In this journey, Rita had won many battles with the application of basic concepts and principles and the knowledge that helping people to fight for justice is the duty of womanhood. She had also learnt that loving one another will connect everyone to one's true self, and will actualise the person to whom he/she really is. But the cross had taught her that nothing comes without sacrifice, self-discipline and courage. As ACT IV, SCENE 3 of Shakespeare's, *Julius Caesar*, emphasised:

> There is a tide in the affairs of men,
> Which, taken at the flood, leads on to fortune;
> Omitted, all the voyage of their life
> Is bound in shallows and in mysteries
> On such a full sea are we now afloat;
> And we must take the current when it serves,
> Or lose our ventures.

With the quote from Shakespeare, Rita's children became an important aspect of her journey. When her husband passed, their support helped her to continue in life. Rita came to understand how motherhood in simultaneous environment could align like the spokes of a wheel. She came to the awareness that it was not only knowing how to turn the wheel to win the race, but turning it in the right direction with love, purpose and connectivity that provides and guides to unearth power. She finally understood that the functions of a pluralistic society in various orbits is greater than human life, and that every person has a journey which has to be travelled gracefully with all truthfulness, happiness, grace and gratitude. Most importantly, helping the family to understand other people's journey helps to keep the shadows in front, giving every love to the family and community. She had learnt that during the journey, she would come across cracks that would widen until they were no more cracks. When this happens, one should not quit, rather one should continue to persevere and press on until that crack forms new shapes and leads to new adventures which would be passed on to the next generation. Rita further understood and imbued in her children the fact that as long as there is life in everyone, there is the need to understand more, because the work of the heart is not done. The best thing to hold onto in life is the love we have for one another at the end, as each person's journey is what will take them to their destination.

Rita's grandchildren brought back a lot of memories and motivated her with their antics to be more playful, vulnerable and free. She came to see what was missing in her life and became overwhelmed with the reality that her family did set her on a new path and this made a great difference in the journey. The children and grandchildren brought her tears of joy, reminding her how keenly alive she was. With them, time became funny and there was never enough time for all of them. She learnt to stretch a moment to an hour and created multiple heights along the expanse of the day. She never saw the possibilities and promises that twenty-four hours actually offered.

The grandchildren became the canvas upon which, like an artist, she created a collage, only to change her mind before the paint dried and compared a new overlapping image with the advent of their next move.

Rita had over the years conditioned her life to adapt to the demands of culture and the ideals of motherhood designing and redesigning her persona. But now, in everything, she was scraping off the surface to have a glimpse of her original self as all the children took the decision for her to retire and take care of herself. She was very fortunate to have all her children around to applaud her progress and help her see whatever stage she was in. Her new project was to accept whatever came with life – pick it up, sift through it and hold onto it. She learnt to accept differences and celebrate the similarities as she watched her new self emerge.

Rita became very delighted with whatever appeared on the journey. The journey had helped her to come to the awareness of how motherhood allows women to be fulfilled in a broader context; accept new possibilities with passion, a trajectory for triumph, and sow seeds for family success.

Rita made every effort to bring all her children and their spouses and her grandchildren to settle in the United States of America. All her children had gotten their university degrees with specialties in different fields of life. Her first son, an engineer and a pentecostal pastor, managed his own church in Virginia. The second son, an electrical engineer, was finishing his doctorate degree in Information Technology and was recognised by the President of the United States of America, President Barak Obama, for his rare achievement in America. The third son, also an engineer from Nigeria who switched to the medical profession in America, had become well known, respected and recognised in the field. Her daughter, a renowned actress with a degree in Theatre Arts from a Nigerian university, became a Certified Registered Nurse in America. Her last son, "The last card", graduated with a Bachelor of Science honours in Psychology from a university in the US, but decided to become more of an international businessman in order to protect and oversee the family property as well as help the poor and powerless back home in Nigeria. Rita had also gotten various degrees – a BSc in Political Science; two master's degrees, one in Education (MEd) and another in Business Administration (MBA) Healthcare Management, Associate Degree in Education and a doctorate degree in Healthcare Management. The cup of motherhood served as a mentor, model and teacher to the family. The touch of motherhood with its vibrance and interrelated experience had helped to propel her children to aim higher in life.

Rita's children were all settled and belonged to their own little world. They held the power of their destiny in their hands. She could only offer advice and wish them Godspeed. With this reality, Rita understood that love blossoms when there is the right amount of tenderness combined with a leash and, in all, vulnerability.

The children were all happy and encouraged their mother to enjoy life; live each day, greet the sun with happiness, wine and dine and generate new ideas. They encouraged her to embrace herself, laugh always because with laughter, one would live longer. Rita had also learnt to meditate on every moment, handing everything over to God, for life is made up of moments. She developed a passion for reading and writing down her thoughts for the next generation. Her children once again encouraged her to become more sensual with life as this was the best attitude towards life.

In this journey, Rita had been embraced by life, tested by its elements, emptied of anxiety and cleansed with fresh thoughts. In the process, she had come to recover what womanhood is. The story of womanhood has made Rita come to realise that God's wonder is always ahead of us but we do not spend enough time thinking about it.

The unfinished journey of womanhood is to acknowledge the fact that work is still in progress and each passage an evolution of experience with the wisdom it offers. Every woman should believe that she can conquer the world no matter her class or background and despite the fact that she is operating in a man's world and trapped in the inspirational energy of this era. One can expedite social change and re-invent oneself as if one had never existed. Today, the journey of motherhood should make every woman proud of who she is, having wisdom, understanding and balance in life.

Rita was very happy and she was not going to allow any unavoidable setbacks overshadow her positive attitude. At the core, she remembered how she often used to strive for perfection in an imperfect world, setting goals and pressures that affected her attitude, relationships, health and wellness. But as she now reconnected with the journey, it reminded her of how many daily lessons the world around us offers.

The womanhood journey signifies that every human born is like a germinated fruit. In the heart of a woman, "the scent of womanhood" is perfumed in each to breathe, and no matter the selfishness and ignorance of a child, as well as how sick he/she is, motherhood arms rock the cradle that holds the human creation which she has brought to the world with love.

As children and while growing up, every human being watches motherhood, looks her straight in the eyes, records her moments, memorises her smiles, traces her frowns and rehearses her moods. Motherhood happens to be each human's heart of happiness from the beginning of life. This was quite obvious to Rita as she watched her grown children become parents and bear their own children, her grandchildren. These young ones ran around her like the ocean's ebb along the shoreline. At night, Rita remembered the grandchildren asking her to hug them to sleep. Their shifting moods as they grew had made her come to realise once again that nothing in this world is permanent; the journey of womanhood is a continuous and an unfinished one.

www.ingramcontent.com/pod-product-compliance
Lightning Source LLC
LaVergne TN
LVHW091601060526
838200LV00036B/945